CONTENTS

Downloadable Maps

Eleven maps used in this book are available for download on our Web site, as well as two color maps: one projection map of the world and one political map of Asia.

How to Download:

1. Go to www.evan-moor.com/resources.

2. Enter your e-mail address and the resource code for this product—EMC3734.

3. You will receive an e-mail with a link to the downloadable maps.

What's in This Book

▶ **5 sections** of reproducible information and activity pages centered on five main topics: Asia in the World, Political Divisions, Physical Features, Valuable Resources, and Culture.

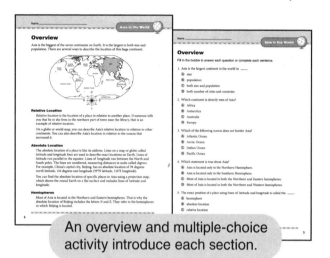

An overview and multiple-choice activity introduce each section.

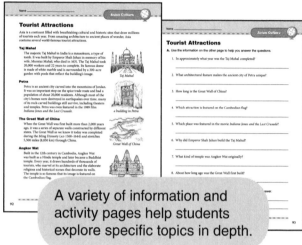

A variety of information and activity pages help students explore specific topics in depth.

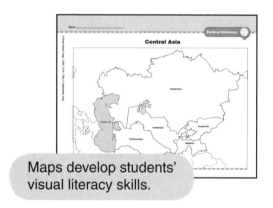

Maps develop students' visual literacy skills.

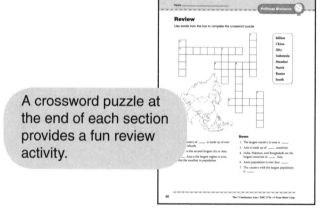

A crossword puzzle at the end of each section provides a fun review activity.

▶ **1 section** of assessment activities

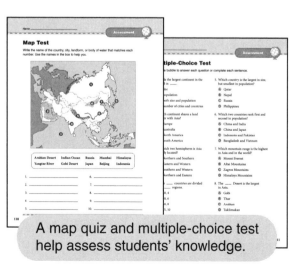

A map quiz and multiple-choice test help assess students' knowledge.

▶ **1 section** of open-ended note takers

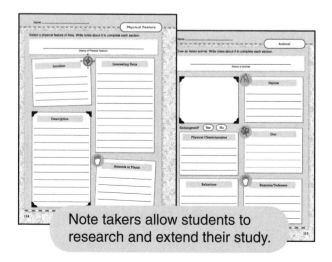

Note takers allow students to research and extend their study.

The 7 Continents: Asia • EMC 3734 • © Evan-Moor Corp.

Asia in the World

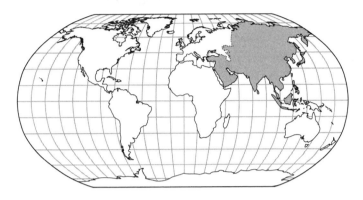

This section introduces students to the location of Asia in the world. Students learn about the difference between relative and absolute location, as well as the hemispheres in which Asia lies. Students also practice using lines of latitude and longitude to find places on a map.

Each skill in this section is based on the following National Geography Standards:

Essential Element 1: The World in Spatial Terms

Standard 1: How to use maps and other geographic representations, tools, and technologies to acquire, process, and report information from a spatial perspective

CONTENTS

Overview

Asia is the biggest of the seven continents on Earth. It is the largest in both size and population. There are several ways to describe the location of this huge continent.

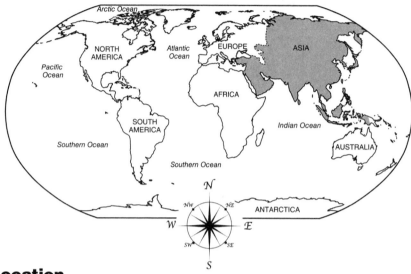

Relative Location

Relative location is the location of a place in relation to another place. If someone tells you that he or she lives in the northern part of town near the library, that is an example of relative location.

On a globe or world map, you can describe Asia's relative location in relation to other continents. You can also describe Asia's location in relation to the oceans that surround it.

Absolute Location

The *absolute location* of a place is like its address. Lines on a map or globe called *latitude* and *longitude lines* are used to describe exact locations on Earth. Lines of latitude run parallel to the equator. Lines of longitude run between the North and South poles. The lines are numbered, measuring distances in units called *degrees*. For example, China's capital city, Beijing, has an absolute location of 39 degrees north latitude, 116 degrees east longitude (39°N latitude, 116°E longitude).

You can find the absolute location of specific places in Asia using a projection map, which shows the round Earth on a flat surface and includes lines of latitude and longitude.

Hemispheres

Most of Asia is located in the Northern and Eastern hemispheres. That is why the absolute location of Beijing includes the letters *N* and *E*. They refer to the hemispheres in which Beijing is located.

Overview

Fill in the bubble to answer each question or complete each sentence.

1. Asia is the largest continent in the world in _____.

   Ⓐ size

   Ⓑ population

   Ⓒ both size and population

   Ⓓ both number of cities and countries

2. Which continent is directly west of Asia?

   Ⓐ Africa

   Ⓑ Antarctica

   Ⓒ Australia

   Ⓓ Europe

3. Which of the following oceans does *not* border Asia?

   Ⓐ Atlantic Ocean

   Ⓑ Arctic Ocean

   Ⓒ Indian Ocean

   Ⓓ Pacific Ocean

4. Which statement is true about Asia?

   Ⓐ Asia is located only in the Northern Hemisphere.

   Ⓑ Asia is located only in the Southern Hemisphere.

   Ⓒ Most of Asia is located in both the Northern and Eastern hemispheres.

   Ⓓ Most of Asia is located in both the Northern and Western hemispheres.

5. The exact position of a place using lines of latitude and longitude is called the _____.

   Ⓐ hemisphere

   Ⓑ absolute location

   Ⓒ relative location

   Ⓓ intermediate direction

Asia's Relative Location

Relative location is the position of a place in relation to another place. How would you describe where Asia is located in the world using relative location?

Look at the world map on the other page. One way to describe Asia's relative location is to name the other continents that border it. For example, Asia is east of Europe and north of Australia. And Central Asia is northeast of Africa.

Another way to describe the relative location of Asia is to name the oceans that surround the continent. The frigid Arctic Ocean borders Asia to the north. To the south is the warm Indian Ocean. The vast Pacific Ocean borders Asia to the east.

A. Use the map on the other page to complete the paragraph about the relative location of Asia.

Asia is the largest continent in the entire world. It is located east of the

continent of _____ and north of the island continent of

_____. Africa is to the _____ of Central Asia.

To the north is the cold _____ Ocean. The Indian Ocean is

_____ of Asia. The _____ Ocean borders the

continent to the east. Asia is a continent that stretches both long and wide.

B. Follow the directions to color the map on the other page.

1. Color the continent west of Asia orange.

2. Use blue to circle the name of the ocean that is east of Asia.

3. Draw a kangaroo next to the island continent south of Asia.

Name

Asia's Relative Location

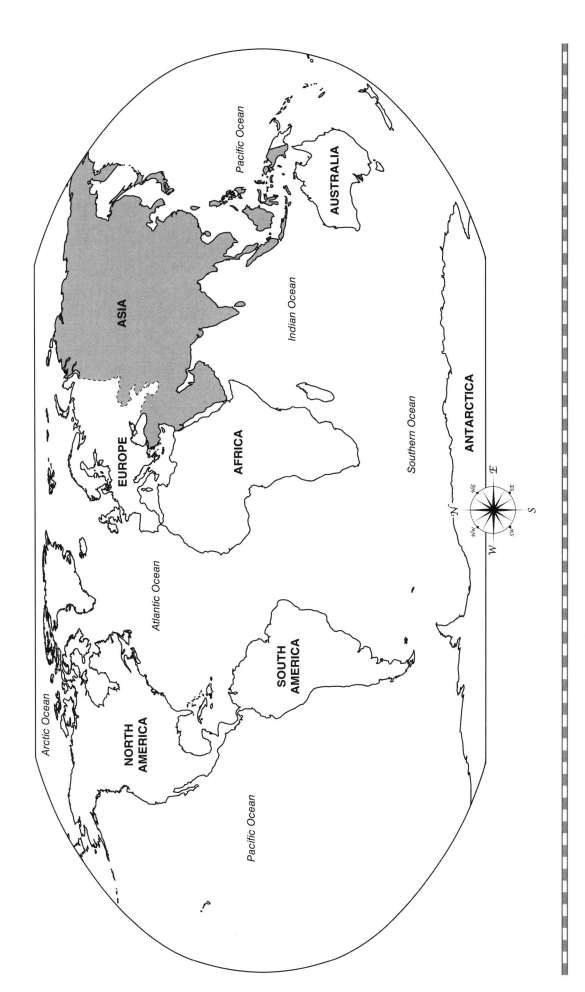

Asia's Hemispheres

On a globe, Earth is divided into four hemispheres by a horizontal line called the *equator* and by vertical lines that run from the North Pole to the South Pole. The hemispheres are the Northern, Southern, Western, and Eastern. Most of Asia is part of the Northern Hemisphere because the majority of the continent is north of the equator. A small part of Asia is located south of the equator, so that part is in the Southern Hemisphere. Asia is also located in the Eastern Hemisphere.

Northern and Southern Hemispheres

A globe shows an imaginary horizontal line that runs around the center of Earth. This line is called the equator. The equator divides Earth into the Northern and Southern hemispheres.

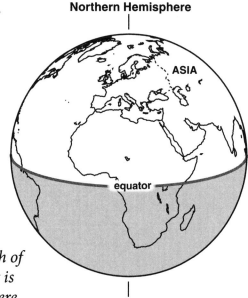

Since most of Asia is north of the equator, the continent is in the Northern Hemisphere.

Western and Eastern Hemispheres

A globe also shows imaginary vertical lines that run from the North Pole to the South Pole. One of these vertical lines is called the *prime meridian*. This line, along with its twin line on the opposite side of the globe, create the Western and Eastern hemispheres.

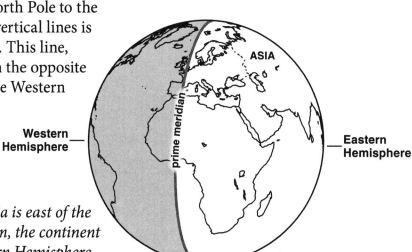

Since all of Asia is east of the prime meridian, the continent is in the Eastern Hemisphere.

Name _____

Asia's Hemispheres

A. Write the letter of the definition that matches each term. Use the information and pictures of the globes on the other page to help you.

_____ 1. Asia

_____ 2. continent

_____ 3. globe

_____ 4. equator

_____ 5. Eastern Hemisphere

_____ 6. hemisphere

_____ 7. North Pole

_____ 8. Northern Hemisphere

_____ 9. prime meridian

a. an imaginary line that runs from the North Pole to the South Pole

b. half of Earth

c. the continent that is mostly in the Northern and Eastern hemispheres

d. the hemisphere that is east of the prime meridian

e. an imaginary line that divides Earth into the Northern and Southern hemispheres

f. any of the seven large landmasses of Earth

g. the northernmost point on Earth

h. a round model of Earth

i. the hemisphere that is north of the equator

B. Label the parts of the globe. Use the letters next to the terms in the box.

A. **Southern Hemisphere**

B. **Asia**

C. **Northern Hemisphere**

D. **Eastern Hemisphere**

E. **equator**

F. **prime meridian**

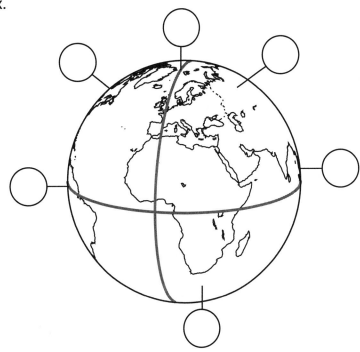

Name _____

Asia's Absolute Location

Many globes contain lines that make it easier to find specific places on Earth. Lines of latitude measure the distance north and south of the equator. Lines of longitude measure the distance east and west of the prime meridian. You can use lines of latitude and longitude to find the absolute location of Asia on a globe.

Latitude

The equator is found at the absolute location of 0° (zero degrees) latitude. Other lines of latitude run parallel to the equator and are labeled with an *N* or *S*, depending on whether they are north or south of the equator. Latitude lines are also called *parallels*.

On the picture of the globe, notice the lines of latitude. Look for the continent of Asia. Since most of the continent is north of the equator, most of the latitude lines used to find the absolute location of places within Asia are labeled in *degrees north*, or °N.

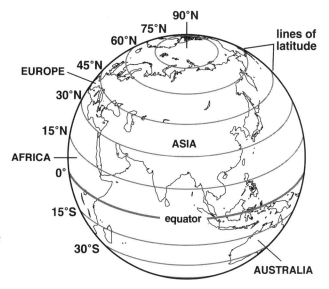

Lines of Latitude (Parallels)

Longitude

The prime meridian runs from the North Pole to the South Pole at 0° (zero degrees) longitude. Other lines of longitude run north and south, too, and are labeled with an *E* or *W*, depending on whether they are east or west of the prime meridian. Longitude lines are also called *meridians*.

On the picture of the globe, notice the lines of longitude. Look for the entire continent of Asia. Since the entire continent is east of the prime meridian, all of the longitude lines used to find the absolute location of places within Asia are labeled in *degrees east*, or °E.

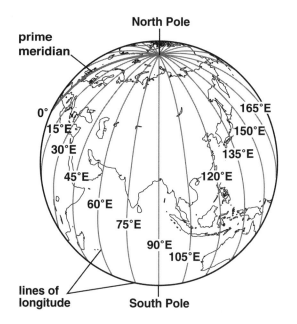

Lines of Longitude (Meridians)

Name _____

Asia's Absolute Location

To find the absolute location of a place, read the latitude line first and then read the longitude line. For example, the latitude 30°N runs through the southern part of China. The longitude 90°E runs through the western part of China. So the absolute location of Southwest China is 30°N latitude, 90°E longitude.

A. Circle the answer to each question. Use the pictures of the globes and information on the other page to help you.

1. Which line is at 0 degrees latitude?   **equator**   **prime meridian**

2. Which line runs north and south?   **equator**   **prime meridian**

3. In which direction is most of Asia from the equator?   **north**   **south**

4. Which line of longitude runs through Asia?   **75°E**   **75°W**

5. Where is the North Pole located?   **90°S**   **90°N**

6. Which lines run parallel to the equator?   **latitude lines**   **longitude lines**

7. How many degrees are between each line of latitude and longitude on the globes?   **10 degrees**   **15 degrees**

8. What is another name for *lines of latitude*?   **meridians**   **parallels**

9. Which line of latitude runs through Asia?   **30°N**   **30°S**

10. What is another name for *lines of longitude*?   **parallels**   **meridians**

B. Using the information on the other page, explain why most places in Asia have absolute locations that are labeled in degrees north and east.

_____

_____

Using a Projection Map

How do you draw a picture of a round object, such as Earth, on a flat piece of paper? In order to show all of Earth's continents and oceans in one view, mapmakers use a system called *projection*. Mapping the round Earth on a flat surface causes some areas to look bigger than they really are. For example, land near the poles gets stretched out when flattened. That's why Greenland and Antarctica look so big on some maps.

A projection map of the world shows all the lines of latitude and longitude on Earth. Study the projection map on the other page. Notice the lines of latitude and longitude. You can use these lines to find the absolute location of a specific place in Asia. For example, the label *Asia* is located at 50°N latitude, 90°E longitude.

A. Read each statement. Circle **yes** if it is true or **no** if it is false. Use the map on the other page to help you.

1. Asia is located on the prime meridian.	**Yes**	**No**
2. Most of Asia is located between the longitudes of 45°E and 170°E.	**Yes**	**No**
3. All of Asia is located between the latitudes of 60°N and 75°N.	**Yes**	**No**
4. Asia is the only continent east of the prime meridian.	**Yes**	**No**
5. Asia shares some of the same north latitude lines with Europe.	**Yes**	**No**
6. The longitude line 90°E runs through Asia and Australia.	**Yes**	**No**
7. The latitude line 30°N runs through Africa and Asia.	**Yes**	**No**
8. Part of Asia is located on the latitude line 30°S.	**Yes**	**No**
9. There are no continents on 60°N latitude.	**Yes**	**No**

B. How many continents can you find on the map that are on the longitude line 120°E? Write their names.

_____

_____

Name

Using a Projection Map

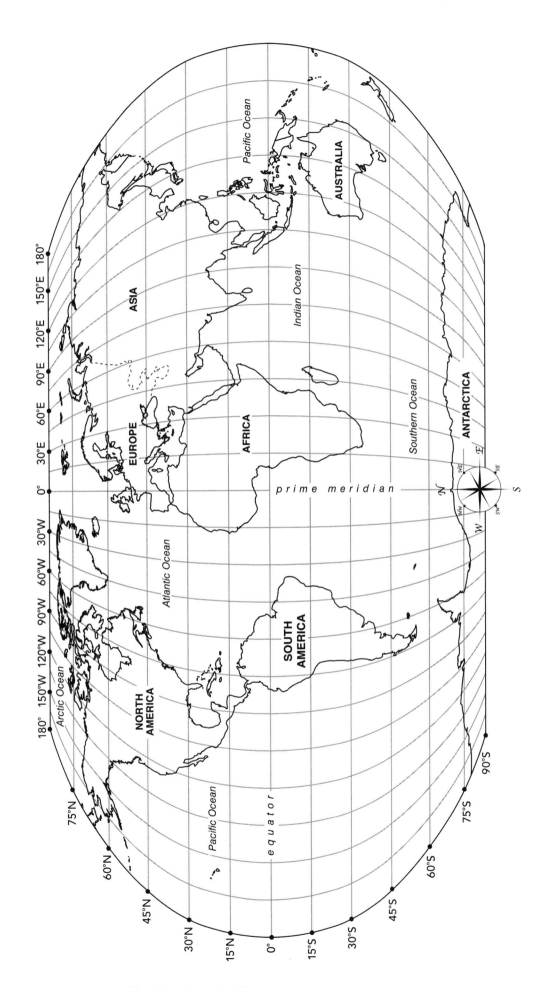

Review

Use words from the box to complete the crossword puzzle.

Africa
Asia
equator
Europe
hemispheres
Pacific
projection
relative

Across

1. The Arctic, Indian, and _____ oceans border Asia.

5. If you go southwest of the center of Asia, you will find the continent of _____.

6. Most of Asia is part of the Northern and Eastern _____.

7. _____ location is a description of a place in relation to another place.

8. The _____ is the imaginary line that divides Earth into the Northern and Southern hemispheres.

Down

2. _____ is the largest continent in the world.

3. The continent of _____ is west of Asia.

4. A _____ map shows the round Earth on a flat surface.

Political Divisions of Asia

This section introduces students to the six regions and 50 countries of Asia. Students learn how the regions differ in size and population, studying data about the largest countries and cities within each region. Students also learn that Asia is now, and will likely continue to be, the most populated continent in the world.

Each skill in this section is based on the following National Geography Standards:

Essential Element 2: Places and Regions

Standard 5: That people create regions to interpret Earth's complexity

Essential Element 4: Human Systems

Standard 9: The characteristics, distribution, and migration of human populations on Earth's surface

CONTENTS

Overview

Asia is the largest continent on Earth in both size and population.

- Asia makes up about 30% of the world's landmass.
- Asia has about 60% of the world's people—4 billion.

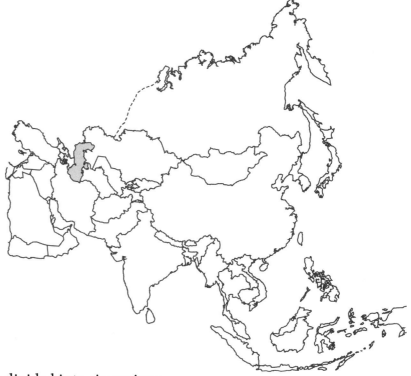

The Six Regions

The 50 countries of Asia are divided into six regions.

Region	Number of Countries	Fast Facts
Southwest Asia	20	also called the Middle East
South Asia	7	includes the second most populated country (India)
Central Asia	5	countries that were once part of Russia
North Asia	1	the largest region in terms of land area
East Asia	6	includes the country with the largest population (China)
Southeast Asia	11	some countries in this region are islands

Where People Live

Most people in Asia live in river valleys or near seacoasts. But Asia also has some of the largest, most densely populated cities in the world. Tokyo, Japan, is the world's most populated metropolitan area. Tokyo has more than 35 million people living in the city and surrounding areas. Some other huge cities are Mumbai, India; Delhi, India; Seoul, South Korea; Shanghai, China; and Jakarta, Indonesia.

Population experts predict that by 2050, the world will have about 9 billion people. Of that 9 billion, over 5 billion will be living in Asia. Asia will retain its ranking as the largest continent in both size and population for a long time.

Name _____

Overview

Fill in the bubble to answer each question or complete each sentence.

1. Asia has ____ countries that are divided into ____ regions.
   - Ⓐ 11, 4
   - Ⓑ 20, 5
   - Ⓒ 35, 6
   - Ⓓ 50, 6

2. Which region of Asia has the most countries?
   - Ⓐ North Asia
   - Ⓑ South Asia
   - Ⓒ Southwest Asia
   - Ⓓ Southeast Asia

3. The north region contains the country of ____.
   - Ⓐ China
   - Ⓑ Russia
   - Ⓒ Indonesia
   - Ⓓ South Korea

4. The most populated metropolitan area in the world is ____.
   - Ⓐ Mumbai, India
   - Ⓑ Tokyo, Japan
   - Ⓒ Shanghai, China
   - Ⓓ Jakarta, Indonesia

5. Which statement is true about Asia's population?
   - Ⓐ Asia has 4 billion people, and it is expected to grow to 5 billion by 2050.
   - Ⓑ Asia has 4 billion people, and it will remain at that number in 2050.
   - Ⓒ Asia has 9 billion people, and it is expected to double in population by 2050.
   - Ⓓ Asia is the largest continent in both size and population, but its ranking will change in 2050.

Name _____

Population of Asia

A *population census* is a survey by a national government to gather information about the number of people who live in a country. Population censuses have been conducted since ancient times. The earliest known population counts were made by the Chinese and Egyptians. Most countries in modern history conduct an official census every 10 years. In addition, experts look at the data from the past to predict what the population will be in the future.

Throughout modern history, Asia has had the largest population of all seven continents. In 1950, Asia's population was about 1.4 billion. By 2010, the population of Asia stood at over 4 billion. By comparison, Africa has the next-largest population of all the continents with about 1 billion people. According to census data, Asia's population will continue to grow steadily, reaching more than 5 billion by 2050.

Asia's Population: 1950–2050

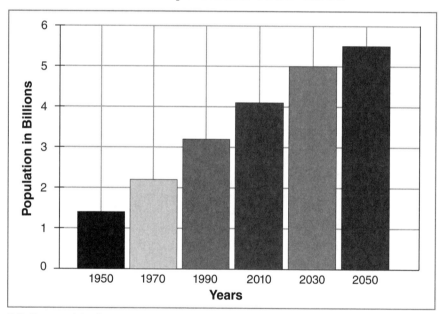

U.S. Bureau of the Census, International Data Base

A. Use the information above to write a caption for the bar graph. Include at least two interesting facts.

_____

_____

_____

Population of Asia

B. Read each statement. Circle **yes** if it is true or **no** if it is false. Use the information on the other page to help you.

1. The graph shows population growth over a 100-year span.   Yes   No

2. In 1950, Asia had a population of exactly 1 billion.   Yes   No

3. From 1950 to 2010, there was a steady increase in population.   Yes   No

4. In 1970, Asia's population jumped to more than 2 billion.   Yes   No

5. In 1990, Asia's population was 4 billion.   Yes   No

6. From 1970 to 1990, Asia's population increased by about 1 billion.   Yes   No

7. Projections show that Asia will have a population of 5 billion in 2030.   Yes   No

8. From 2030 to 2050, Asia's population will decrease by 500 million.   Yes   No

9. The bar graph shows population growth figures in 20-year segments.   Yes   No

10. The bar graph shows that after 2050, Asia's population will start to decrease.   Yes   No

C. Use the information in the bar graph to answer the questions. Circle the answer.

1. During which 20-year period did the population increase the most?

    1950–1970   **1970–1990**   **1990–2010**

2. What would you predict the population of Asia to be in 2070?

    8 billion   **less than 5 billion**   **more than 6 billion**

Name _____

Countries of Asia

Asia is made up of 50 countries. Some are large in population. China and India are the most populated countries of Asia. Some countries are large in size, such as Russia and China. And some are small island nations, such as Brunei and Timor-Leste.

A. Read the names of the Asian countries. Notice there are asterisks (*) after four countries. Read the footnotes below the list to learn how these countries are unique.

Afghanistan	Indonesia	Mongolia	Sri Lanka
Armenia	Iran	Myanmar (Burma)	Syria
Azerbaijan	Iraq	Nepal	Taiwan***
Bahrain	Israel	North Korea	Tajikistan
Bangladesh	Japan	Oman	Thailand
Bhutan	Jordan	Pakistan	Timor-Leste (East Timor)
Brunei	Kazakhstan	Philippines	Turkey**
Cambodia	Kuwait	Qatar	Turkmenistan
China	Kyrgyzstan	Russia**	United Arab Emirates (UAE)
Cyprus	Laos	Saudi Arabia	Uzbekistan
Egypt*	Lebanon	Singapore	Vietnam
Georgia	Malaysia	South Korea	Yemen
India	Maldives		

* The country of Egypt is also included on the list of countries in Africa. Egypt lies mostly in Africa. However, the northeast corner of Egypt is called the Sinai Peninsula. The Sinai Peninsula is considered part of Southwest Asia.

** The countries of Russia and Turkey lie mostly in Asia, so they have been included in the total number of Asian countries. However, parts of these countries also lie in Europe.

*** It is disputed whether Taiwan is an independent country. Taiwan considers itself an independent country. China claims that Taiwan is part of China.

B. Look at the political map of Asia on the other page. Find the following five countries and color each one a different color.

Mongolia	**South Korea**	**Sri Lanka**	**Turkey**	**Yemen**

Name _____

Countries of Asia

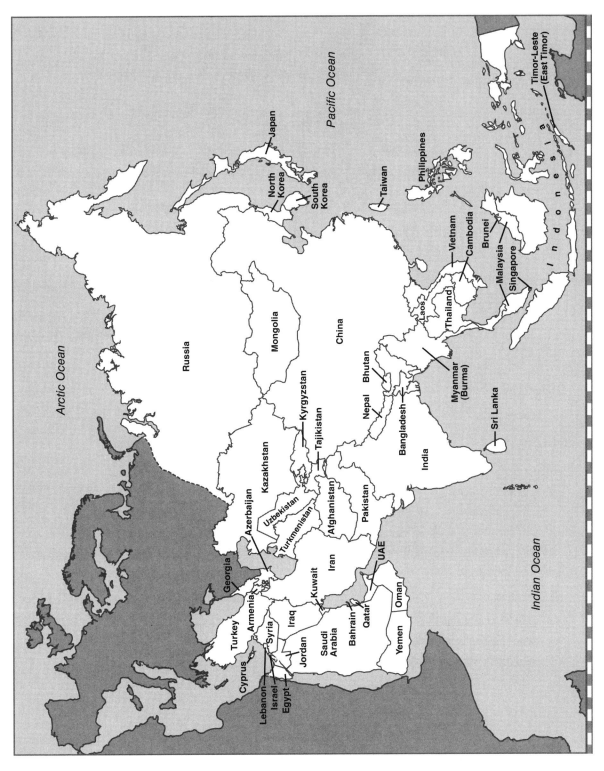

Largest Countries by Area

Asia has some of the world's largest countries in terms of square miles (or kilometers). In fact, of the 10 largest countries in the world, four are located in Asia.

The five largest countries of Asia (listed in alphabetical order) are:

China:	3,705,407 square miles	(9,596,961 square km)
India:	1,269,219 square miles	(3,287,263 square km)
Kazakhstan:	1,052,090 square miles	(2,724,900 square km)
Russia (Asian part):	4,937,800 square miles	(12,788,842 square km)
Saudi Arabia:	830,000 square miles	(2,149,690 square km)

A. Fill in the chart to rank the five largest countries from **1** to **5**, with **1** being the largest.

Rank in Size	Country	Square Miles	Square Kilometers
1			
2			
3			
4			
5			

B. On the map on the other page, you will see five numbered countries. The numbers indicate the rank of each country according to size. Color each country a different color. Then complete the map key by writing the country names in order from largest to smallest. Write the color you used on the map for each country.

Largest Countries by Area

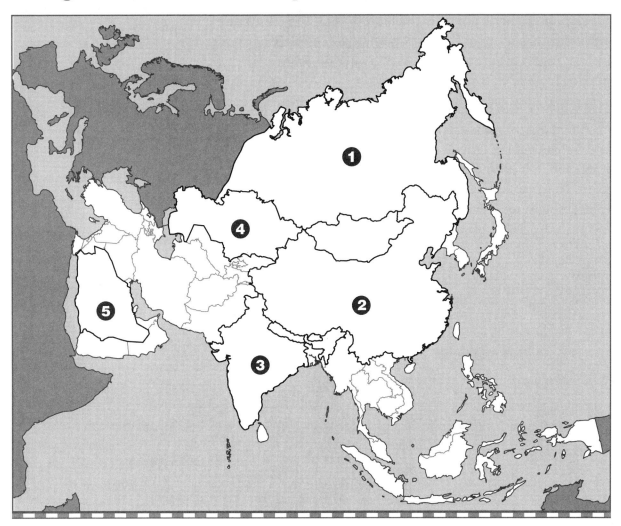

MAP KEY

The Five Largest Countries   **Color**

1. _____   _____

2. _____   _____

3. _____   _____

4. _____   _____

5. _____   _____

Largest Countries by Population

Asia's population is not only the largest of all the continents, but it also has some of the most populated countries. In fact, both China and India have bigger populations than the entire continent of Africa!

Two ways to read large population numbers are by standard form and by word form. For example, 1,355,350,000 is written in standard form. In word form, the number is written out like this: 1 billion, 355 million, 350 thousand.

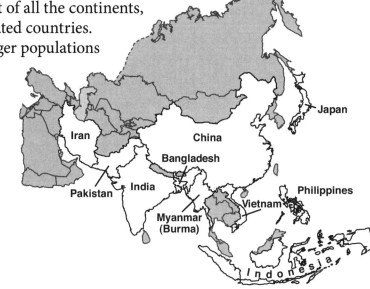

Most Populated Countries of Asia

Rank	Country	Population
1	China	1,355,350,000 (1 billion, 355 million, 350 thousand)
2	India	1,202,135,000 (1 billion, 202 million, 135 thousand)
3	Indonesia	237,383,000 (237 million, 383 thousand)
4	Pakistan	173,117,000 (173 million, 117 thousand)
5	Bangladesh	161,315,000 (161 million, 315 thousand)
6	Japan	127,669,000 (127 million, 669 thousand)
7	Philippines	93,715,000 (93 million, 715 thousand)
8	Vietnam	88,257,000 (88 million, 257 thousand)
9	Iran	74,131,000 (74 million, 131 thousand)
10	Myanmar	50,053,000 (50 million, 53 thousand)

Populations are 2010 estimates based on figures from official government and United Nations sources.

Largest Countries by Population

A. Look at the chart on the other page. Notice that the population figures are written in both standard form and word form. Use the information in the chart to answer the questions.

1. How many countries have a population of over 1 billion? _____

2. Which country has a population of 74 million, 131 thousand? _____

3. How many countries have a population of under 100,000,000? _____

4. What is the population of Japan? Write it in word form.

   _____

5. Which countries rank 1st and 10th in population?

   1st: _____   10th: _____

6. Which country has a population of 173,117,000? _____

7. What is the difference in population between China and _____
   India? Write the answer in standard form.

8. As of 2010, the U.S. population was about 308,000,000. How many Asian
   countries in the chart have more people than the U.S.? How many have
   fewer people than the U.S.?

   More: _____   Fewer: _____

B. When reading the chart on the other page, remember that population figures
are always changing. The population figures on that page are for 2010. Go to the
U.S. Census Bureau Web site to see the second-by-second population clocks.
As of the day this was written, the U.S. population was 308,116,814 and changing
every second. The world population was 6,802,278,428.

   What is the U.S. population right now? _____

   What is the world population right now? _____

Southwest Asia

Southwest Asia is a region that is made up of 20 countries. Sometimes this region is called the Middle East. Some countries in this region are large in size, such as Saudi Arabia, Iran, and Turkey. Some are very small, such as Cyprus, Lebanon, and Qatar.

About 330 million people live in Southwest Asia. The most populated countries completely within Asia's boundaries are Afghanistan, Iran, Iraq, and Saudi Arabia.

Some well-known cities in this region include Baghdad, Iraq; Istanbul, Turkey; Riyadh, Saudi Arabia; and Tel Aviv, Israel.

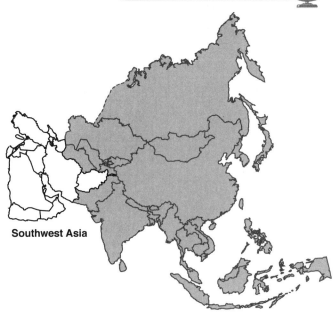

Southwest Asia

A. Find and circle the names of the Southwest Asian countries in the word search. Words may appear across, down, or diagonally.

```
U  D  J  U  H  C  J  Q  N  H  E  U  L  U  A
T  E  G  J  I  A  A  J  Y  L  Y  O  Q  B  F
H  F  N  Y  S  R  A  S  V  K  J  I  B  C  G
L  W  M  A  R  V  H  R  I  F  L  K  R  U  H
D  K  V  Z  A  R  S  Y  R  I  A  O  D  A  A
T  L  A  U  E  S  A  Q  A  W  I  F  U  F  N
L  T  V  L  L  B  I  S  Q  L  W  L  Q  U  I
J  C  K  J  S  F  F  N  K  U  W  A  I  T  S
Y  O  K  E  Y  T  L  M  A  G  L  T  K  C  T
R  Q  R  T  U  R  K  E  Y  H  Q  F  T  M  A
V  J  W  D  T  J  W  R  Y  W  G  K  C  O  N
N  O  K  E  A  R  S  I  Z  T  K  F  A  N  U
K  T  V  I  P  N  N  V  Z  Q  L  G  A  X  K
D  K  T  S  N  G  A  O  L  H  J  Q  A  P  Y
J  P  A  R  I  N  M  V  R  D  T  Q  D  P  O
```

| Afghanistan |
| Iran |
| Iraq |
| Israel |
| Jordan |
| Kuwait |
| Syria |
| Turkey |

Southwest Asia

B. Look at the map of Southwest Asia. Color all 20 countries. Then write a paragraph about the region on the lines. Use the information on the other page to help you.

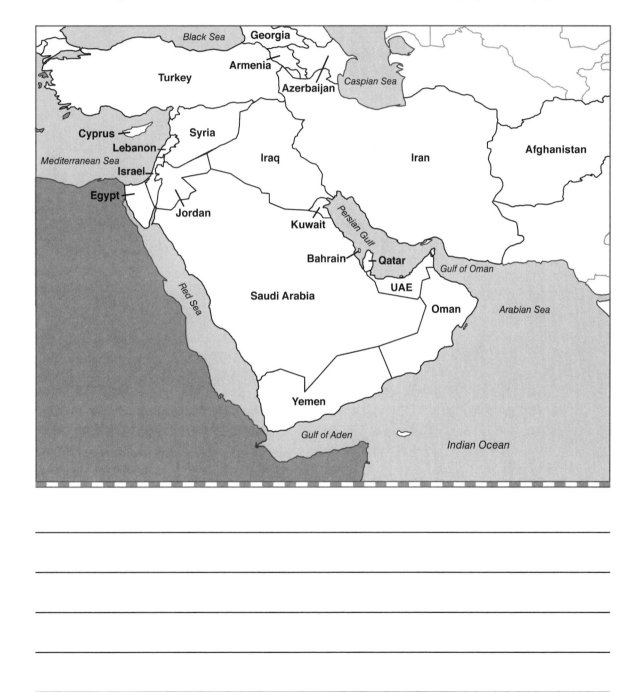

_____

_____

_____

_____

_____

South Asia

South Asia is a region that is made up of seven countries. India, Pakistan, and Bangladesh are the largest in population. The other four countries—Bhutan, Nepal, the Maldives, and Sri Lanka—have large populations, too, but are very small in size.

South Asia is one of the world's most crowded regions. The area has a population of about 1.5 billion. India has the largest population within this region. It is home to more than 1 billion people.

There are several huge, crowded cities in South Asia. Mumbai, India, is one of the largest cities in the world. It has a population of nearly 12 million.

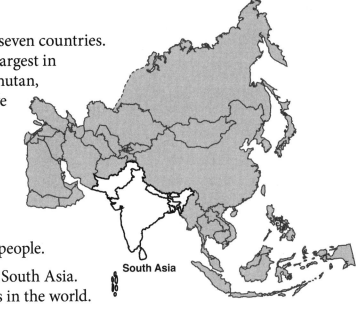

South Asia

A. Complete each sentence by unscrambling the word under the line. Use the information above and the map of South Asia on the other page to help you.

1. South Asia is made up of seven _____.
   setociunr

2. This region is home to more than 1.5 _____ people.
   lboinil

3. The country of _____ has the largest population.
   diina

4. Pakistan is the _____-largest country in size in South Asia.
   ecsnod

5. The largest city in this region is _____.
   baimum

6. The _____ is a country made up of small islands.
   ldviemsa

7. The countries of Pakistan, Nepal, Bhutan, and _____ each share a border with India.
   angaldsehb

8. The island nation of _____ is found off the southern tip of India.
   ris kalan

South Asia

B. On the map below, use blue to circle the Maldives. Then color each of the other countries a different color. Write three facts about South Asia on the lines under the map. Use the information on the other page to help you.

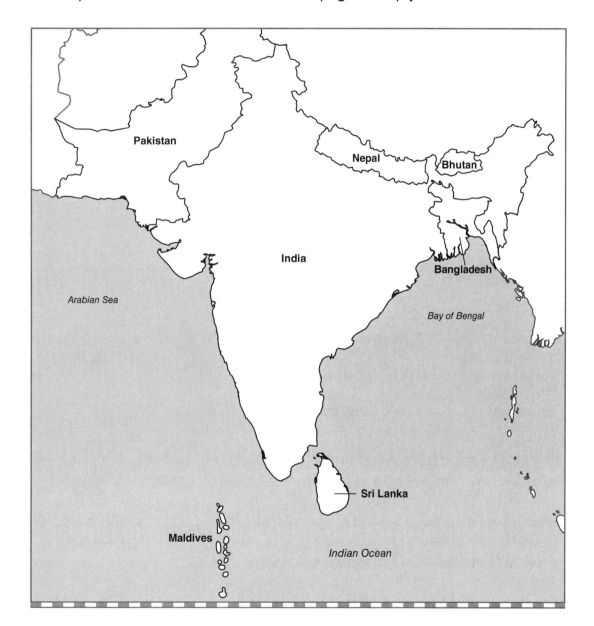

1. _____

2. _____

3. _____

Central Asia

Central Asia is made up of five countries. They are Kazakhstan, Kyrgyzstan, Tajikistan, Turkmenistan, and Uzbekistan. (See activity A for pronunciations.) The region is large in size but has a smaller population than other parts of Asia.

About 93 million people, or about 2% of Asia's population, live in Central Asia. Uzbekistan has the largest population, with more than 28 million. The city of Tashkent, Uzbekistan, is the largest in the region. More than 2 million people live in Tashkent.

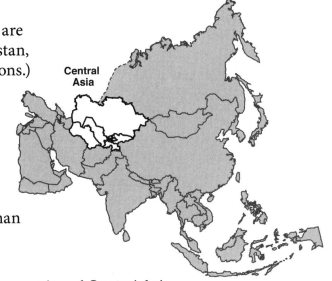

Central Asia

A. The following is a pronunciation key for the countries of Central Asia. Practice saying the country names out loud.

1. Kazakhstan: KAH-zahk-stahn

2. Kyrgyzstan: KEER-ghi-stan

3. Tajikistan: tah-JIK-ih-stan

4. Turkmenistan: turk-MEN-ih-stan

5. Uzbekistan: ooz-BEK-ih-stan

B. Read each question. Fill in the letters to complete the name of the country. Use the information above and the map of Central Asia on the other page to help you.

1. Which country is the largest in size?   — — — — — — **stan**

2. Which country has the largest population?   — — — — — — **stan**

3. The Caspian Sea borders Kazakhstan and which other country?   — — — — — — — — **stan**

4. Which country does *not* border Kazakhstan?   — — — — — — **stan**

5. Tajikistan and which other country are the smallest in size?   — — — — — **stan**

Central Asia

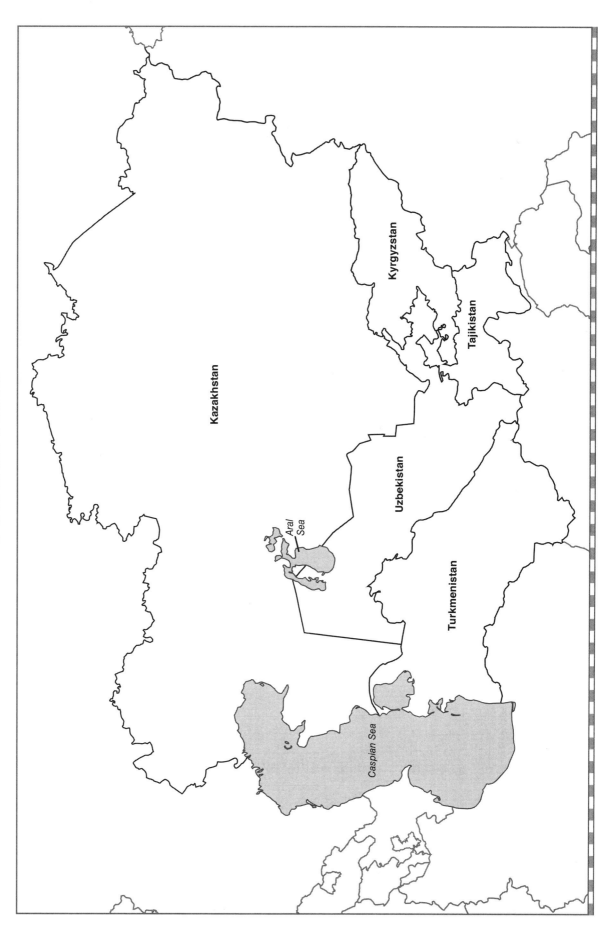

Kazakhstan

Kyrgyzstan

Tajikistan

Uzbekistan

Aral Sea

Turkmenistan

Caspian Sea

North Asia

North Asia is the largest region in Asia, stretching from the Ural Mountains near Europe to the Pacific Ocean in the east. This vast, cold region covers about 30% of the continent. North Asia is also called Siberia.

The region is unique because it contains only one country—Russia. Russia is so large that three-fourths of it lies in Asia and one-fourth of it lies in Europe.

North Asia

Although North Asia is the largest region, it has the smallest population. About 37 million people live in Asian Russia. That is only 1% of Asia's total population. Novosibirsk (Noh-vih-suh-BEERSK) is the largest city in North Asia, with a population of about 1.5 million.

A. Write the missing words on the lines. Use the information above to help you. Then read the paragraphs aloud to a partner.

North Asia is the largest _____ in Asia. Another

name for the vast, cold region of North Asia is _____.

It covers about _____% of the continent. Although North Asia is the

largest region, it has the smallest _____.

Russia is the only _____ in North Asia. Russia is so

large that three-fourths of it lies in Asia and one-fourth lies on the continent

of _____. The _____ Mountains

form the border between Asian Russia and European Russia. About 37 million

people live in Asian Russia. The most populated city in Asian Russian is

_____, with a population of about 1.5 million.

North Asia

B. Color Asian Russia your favorite color. Then write a paragraph about North Asia on the lines. Use the information on the other page to help you.

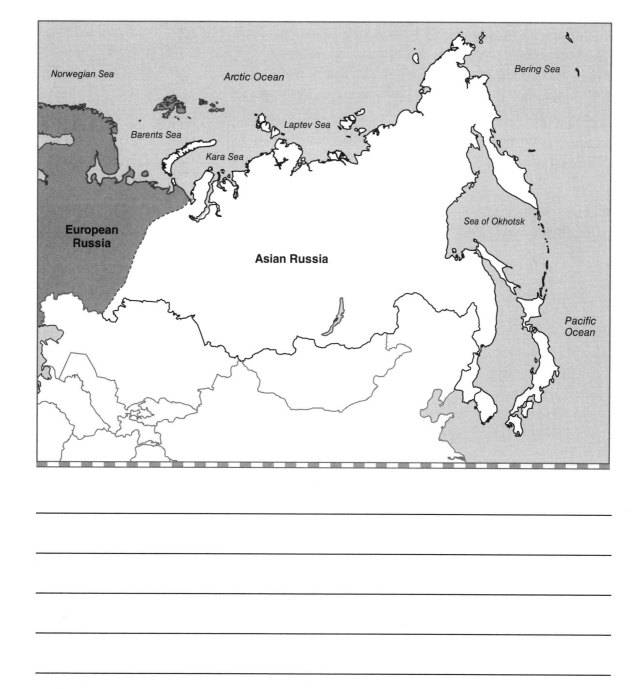

_____

_____

_____

_____

_____

_____

East Asia

East Asia is made up of six countries. They are China, Japan, North Korea, South Korea, Mongolia, and Taiwan. China is the largest, covering 90% of East Asia.

More than 1.5 billion people, or 40% of all Asians, live in East Asia. China has the largest population of any country—not only in Asia, but also in the world. It has more than 100 cities that each have over 1 million people.

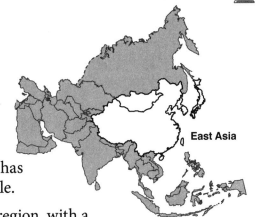

East Asia

Beijing, China, is one of the largest capital cities in the region, with a population of more than 11 million. Seoul, South Korea, is another large capital city, with over 10 million residents.

A. Look at the chart of East Asian countries and their capital cities, in order from highest population to lowest. Use the information in the chart to answer the questions below.

Country	Capital	Population
China	Beijing	11,510,000
South Korea	Seoul	10,422,000
Japan	Tokyo	8,490,000
North Korea	Pyongyang	2,700,000
Taiwan	Taipei	2,600,000
Mongolia	Ulaanbaatar	980,000

1. Which capital has the largest population? _____

2. Which capital has the smallest population? _____

3. What is the capital city of South Korea? _____

4. Tokyo is the capital of which country? _____

5. Which capital—Pyongyang or Taipei—has the larger population? _____

B. Using the map of East Asia on the other page, write the name of each country's capital city next to the star. Use the chart on this page to help you. Then color each country a different color.

East Asia

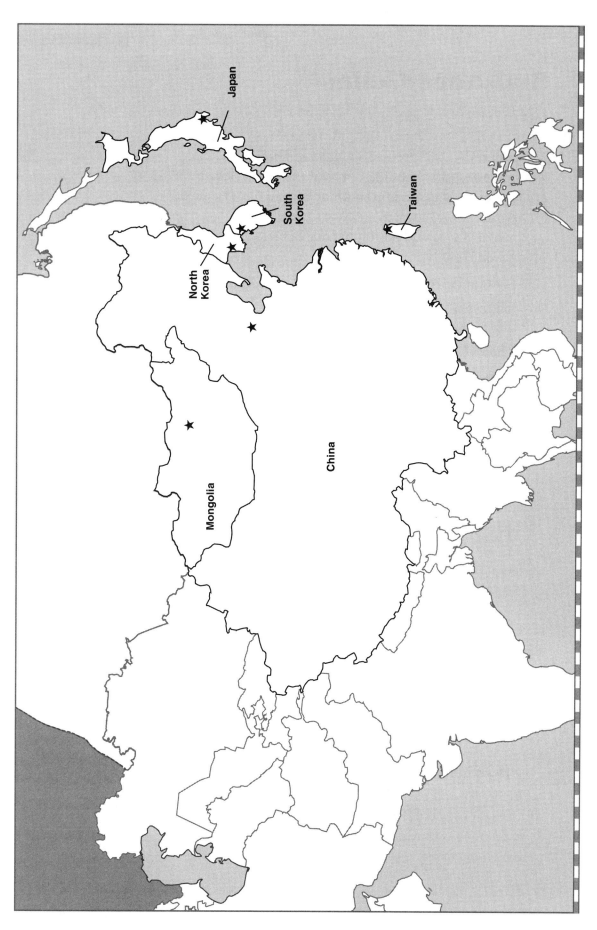

Japan

Taiwan

South Korea

North Korea

Mongolia

China

Southeast Asia

Eleven countries make up the region of Southeast Asia. They are Brunei, Cambodia, Indonesia, Laos, Malaysia, Myanmar, the Philippines, Singapore, Thailand, Timor-Leste, and Vietnam. Some of the countries are located on a peninsula south of China. Others are island nations located south and east of the peninsula. The island nation of Indonesia is made up of over 17,500 islands!

Southeast
Asia

The population of the region is about 539 million. Two of the largest cities are the capital cities of Jakarta, Indonesia, and Bangkok, Thailand. Jakarta has more than 8 million people, and Bangkok has more than 6 million.

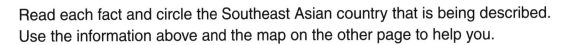

Read each fact and circle the Southeast Asian country that is being described. Use the information above and the map on the other page to help you.

1. This country is made up of over 17,500 islands.   **Indonesia**   **Singapore**

2. Bangkok is the capital of this country.   **Myanmar**   **Thailand**

3. This country does *not* border the ocean.   **Timor-Leste**   **Laos**

4. This country is located on a peninsula.   **Cambodia**   **Philippines**

5. This country is the smallest in size.   **Singapore**   **Vietnam**

6. This island nation is east of Vietnam.   **Malaysia**   **Philippines**

7. Malaysia is on the same island as this country.   **Brunei**   **Timor-Leste**

8. This country borders the Gulf of Tonkin.   **Laos**   **Vietnam**

9. The Gulf of Thailand borders this country.   **Indonesia**   **Thailand**

10. Singapore is off the coast of this country.   **Myanmar**   **Malaysia**

Name _____

Southeast Asia

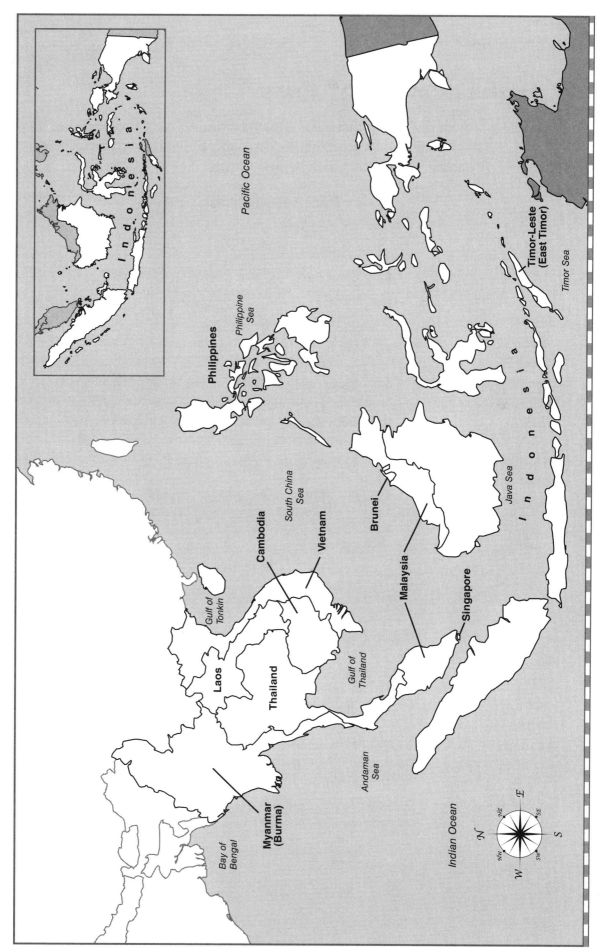

Pacific Ocean

Indonesia

Timor-Leste
(East Timor)

Timor Sea

Philippines

Philippine
Sea

South China
Sea

Gulf of
Tonkin

Cambodia

Vietnam

Brunei

Malaysia

Singapore

Indonesia

Java Sea

Laos

Thailand

Gulf of
Thailand

Andaman
Sea

Myanmar
(Burma)

Bay of
Bengal

Indian Ocean

N

NW NE

W   E

SW SE

S

Largest Cities of Asia

Asia is a continent filled with densely populated cities. In fact, Asia has 14 of the 20 largest cities in the world, including the three most populated cities on Earth: Shanghai, China; Mumbai, India; and Beijing, China.

Most Populated Cities of Asia

Rank	City	Country	Population
1	Shanghai	China	14,349,000
2	Mumbai	India	11,915,000
3	Beijing	China	11,510,000
4	Seoul	South Korea	10,422,000
5	Delhi	India	9,817,439
6	Chongqing	China	9,692,000
7	Istanbul	Turkey	9,556,000
8	Karachi	Pakistan	9,339,000
9	Jakarta	Indonesia	8,640,000
10	Guangzhou	China	8,525,000
11	Tokyo	Japan	8,490,000
12	Tianjin	China	7,499,000
13	Tehran	Iran	7,189,000
14	Hong Kong	China	6,857,000
15	Bangkok	Thailand	5,659,000

Populations are estimates based on figures from official government and United Nations sources.

The 7 Continents: Asia • EMC 3734 • © Evan-Moor Corp.

Largest Cities of Asia

A. Circle the answer to each question. Use the chart on the other page to help you.

1. Which city has the larger population?   **Mumbai**   **Delhi**

2. What is the difference in population between Jarkarta and Guangzhou?   **1,115,000**   **115,000**

3. In which country is Tehran located?   **Iran**   **India**

4. Which city is in the top five most populated cities of Asia?   **Seoul**   **Istanbul**

5. How many of the top 15 cities are located in China?   **four**   **six**

6. Which city has a population of about 9.3 million?   **Tokyo**   **Karachi**

7. What is the difference in population between the largest and 15th-largest cities?   **less than 10 million**   **more than 10 million**

B. New York City is the most populated city in the United States, with about 8,364,000 people. Use this information, as well as the chart on the other page, to answer the questions.

1. How many Asian cities have a higher population than New York City?   _____

2. How many more people does Shanghai have than New York City? Write your answer in standard form.   _____

3. Name the Asian cities in the chart that have fewer people than New York City.

    _____

Review

Use words from the box to complete the crossword puzzle.

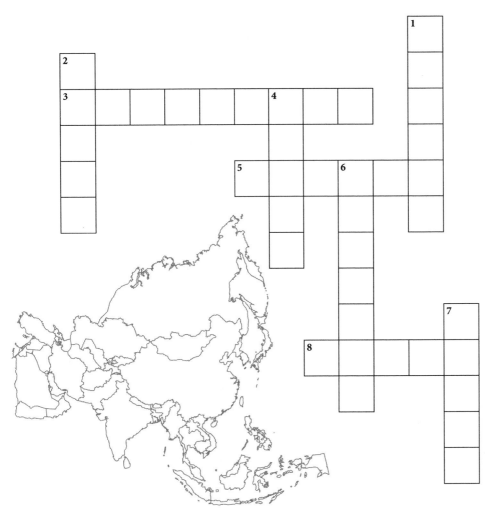

| billion |
| China |
| fifty |
| Indonesia |
| Mumbai |
| North |
| Russia |
| South |

Across

3. The country of _____ is made up of over 17,500 islands.

5. _____ is the second-largest city in Asia.

8. _____ Asia is the largest region in area, but the smallest in population.

Down

1. The largest country in area is _____.

2. Asia is made up of _____ countries.

4. India, Pakistan, and Bangladesh are the largest countries in _____ Asia.

6. Asia's population is over four _____.

7. The country with the largest population is _____.

Physical Features of Asia

This section introduces students to the landforms and bodies of water of Asia. Students discover that Asia's landscape includes rugged mountains, dry deserts, vast plains, lush forests, and thousands of islands, as well as many of the world's largest rivers, lakes, and inland seas. Students also become familiar with the oceans, seas, bays, and gulfs that surround Asia.

Each skill in this section is based on the following National Geography Standards:

Essential Element 2: Places and Regions

Standard 4: The physical and human characteristics of places

Essential Element 3: Physical Systems

Standards 7 & 8: The physical processes that shape the patterns of Earth's surface; the characteristics and spatial distribution of ecosystems on Earth's surface

CONTENTS

Overview

Asia is the world's largest continent. It is part of the same landmass as Europe—no body of water separates the two continents completely.

Asia has some of the world's largest and most famous landforms and bodies of water.

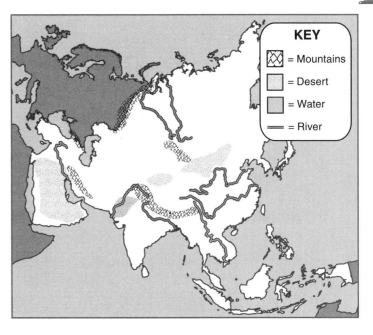

KEY
⊠ = Mountains
▢ = Desert
▤ = Water
— = River

Landforms

Asia has more mountains than any other continent. The highest mountain range in the world, the Himalayas, is located in Asia. And the world's highest mountain, Mount Everest, is in the Himalayas.

Asia also has large, barren deserts. Asia's largest desert, the Arabian Desert, is hot and sandy. The second-largest desert in Asia is the Gobi Desert, which is colder and has some grassland.

Plains and plateaus make up much of northern Asia. The West Siberian Plain is the largest level region in the world. The Central Siberian Plateau and the East Siberian Uplands also stretch across this region of Asia.

In the far east, Asia becomes a continent of thousands of islands. Japan, the Philippines, and Indonesia are just three of its island nations.

Bodies of Water

Asia is a continent surrounded by and filled with many large and famous bodies of water. It is bordered on three sides by the Arctic, Indian, and Pacific oceans. It is also surrounded by many seas, including the Arabian Sea, Bering Sea, and Red Sea.

Inland, there are several bodies of water. The Caspian Sea is the world's largest inland body of water, and is actually a salt lake. The Dead Sea in the Middle East is the lowest place on Earth. The largest freshwater lake in the world is Lake Baikal in Russia.

Several long, winding rivers flow through Asia, including the Yangtze (Chang Jiang) River, which is the longest river in Asia. Other long rivers are the Ganges, Indus, and Mekong rivers.

Name _____

Overview

Fill in the bubble to answer each question or complete each sentence.

1. Mount Everest is found in the ____.
   - Ⓐ Ural Mountains
   - Ⓑ Himalayas
   - Ⓒ Arabian Desert
   - Ⓓ Central Siberian Plateau

2. The Gobi is the second-largest ____ in Asia.
   - Ⓐ plain
   - Ⓑ plateau
   - Ⓒ sea
   - Ⓓ desert

3. Which sea does *not* border Asia?
   - Ⓐ Arabian Sea
   - Ⓑ Bering Sea
   - Ⓒ Caribbean Sea
   - Ⓓ Red Sea

4. Which statement is true?
   - Ⓐ The Dead Sea is the lowest place on Earth.
   - Ⓑ The Caspian Sea is a freshwater lake.
   - Ⓒ Lake Baikal is actually a salt lake.
   - Ⓓ The Arabian Sea is the world's largest inland body of water.

5. The ____, or ____, is the longest river in Asia.
   - Ⓐ Indus, Ganges
   - Ⓑ Ganges, Mekong
   - Ⓒ Yangtze, Chang Jiang
   - Ⓓ Chang Jiang, Mekong

Asia's Diverse Landscape

Much of Asia's land is rugged, meaning it has rough terrain. The continent features high mountains, grassy plains, frozen tundra, and barren deserts. But Asia also has lush forests ranging from dense *coniferous*, or evergreen, forests in Russia to tropical rainforests in the southeast. With a continent this large, it's no wonder that the landscape is so diverse.

A. Look at the physical map of Asia on the other page. Use the map to answer the questions.

1. Which desert is between the Altay Mountains and the Manchurian Plain? _____

2. What is the name of the major peak shown on the map? _____

3. What kind of landform makes up the Arabian Peninsula? _____

4. Which mountain range helps form the northwestern border of Asia? _____

5. What is the name of the plain that is between the Ob and Yenisei rivers? _____

6. In which direction are the Altay Mountains from the Himalayas? _____

7. Which plateau is located south of the Himalayas? _____

8. What is the name of the landform that is east of the Gobi Desert? _____

B. Read the directions to color the map on the other page.

1. Color the mountains brown.

2. Color the deserts yellow.

3. Use blue to outline the rivers.

4. Use green to circle the names of the plains and plateaus.

Name

Asia's Diverse Landscape

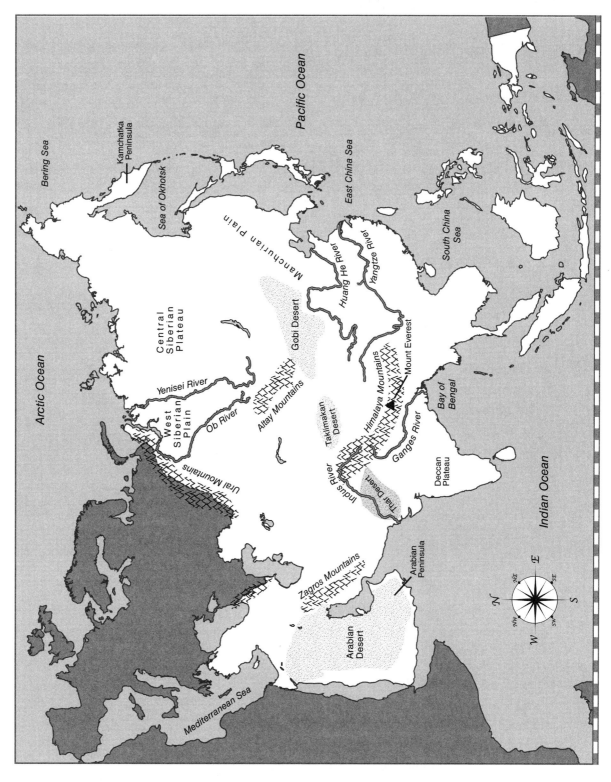

Arctic Ocean

Bering Sea

Kamchatka Peninsula

Sea of Okhotsk

Pacific Ocean

Manchurian Plain

East China Sea

Central Siberian Plateau

Gobi Desert

Huang He River

Yangtze River

South China Sea

Yenisei River

Altay Mountains

Himalaya Mountains

Mount Everest

Bay of Bengal

West Siberian Plain

Ob River

Taklimakan Desert

Ural Mountains

Indus River

Ganges River

Thar Desert

Deccan Plateau

Indian Ocean

Zagros Mountains

Arabian Peninsula

Arabian Desert

Mediterranean Sea

N NE E SE S SW W NW

The Himalayas

With several peaks towering above 27,000 feet, the Himalayas are the world's highest mountains. They lie between India and China.

Facts About the Himalayas

- *Himalaya* means "house of snow," or "snowy range" in Sanskrit, an ancient language of India.

- The highest peak in the Himalayas is Mount Everest, which is located on the border of Tibet and Nepal.

- The mountain system is about 1,491 miles (2,400 km) in length, which makes it the third-longest system of mountains in the world.

- Five countries border the Himalayas—Bhutan, India, Nepal, Pakistan, and the Tibetan part of China.

- There are about 15,000 glaciers throughout the Himalayas.

- Ten of Asia's largest rivers flow down from the Himalayas.

- Despite the harsh conditions and high elevations, the Himalayas still provide a habitat for a variety of animals, including wild yak, red pandas, snow leopards, and Himalayan black bears.

There are more than 100 mountains that are over 23,600 feet high in the Himalayas. Below are the 10 highest peaks of the mountain range.

Highest Himalayan Peaks

Rank	Mountain Peak	Location	Height in Feet (Meters)
1	Everest	Nepal/Tibet	29,035 feet (8,850 m)
2	K2	Pakistan/China	28,250 feet (8,611 m)
3	Kanchenjunga	Nepal/India	28,169 feet (8,586 m)
4	Lhotse	Nepal/Tibet	27,940 feet (8,516 m)
5	Makalu	Nepal/Tibet	27,766 feet (8,463 m)
6	Cho Oyu	Nepal/Tibet	26,906 feet (8,201 m)
7	Dhaulagiri	Nepal	26,795 feet (8,167 m)
8	Manaslu	Nepal	26,781 feet (8,163 m)
9	Nanga Parbat	Pakistan	26,660 feet (8,126 m)
10	Annapurna	Nepal	26,545 feet (8,091 m)

The 7 Continents: Asia • EMC 3734 • © Evan-Moor Corp.

The Himalayas

A. Read each statement. Circle **yes** if it is true or **no** if it is false. Use the information on the other page to help you.

1. The Himalayas border six countries in Asia.   Yes   No

2. The Himalayan mountain range is the longest in the world.   Yes   No

3. Major Asian rivers flow from the Himalaya Mountains.   Yes   No

4. Even though the Himalayas are snow-covered, there are no glaciers.   Yes   No

5. All of the 10 highest mountain peaks are located in Nepal or Tibet.   Yes   No

6. K2 is the second-highest mountain peak in the Himalayas.   Yes   No

7. Mount Everest is 28,250 feet (8,611 m) high.   Yes   No

8. There are only 10 mountains in the Himalayas that are higher than 23,600 feet. Yes   No

9. Of the 10 highest mountain peaks, four of them border both Nepal and Tibet.   Yes   No

10. The third-highest mountain peak is Kanchenjunga at 28,169 feet (8,586 m).   Yes   No

B. Circle the correct answer under each question. Use the chart on the other page to help you.

1. What is the difference in feet between the highest and the tenth-highest mountains in the Himalayas?

   about 2,500 feet   **about 250 feet**   **about 25 feet**

2. How many meters taller is Lhotse than Dhaulagiri?

   96 meters   **196 meters**   **349 meters**

Trek to the Summit of Everest

For most mountain climbers, the ultimate experience is to climb to the *summit*, or highest point, of Mount Everest. The first trip to the summit was by Sir Edmund Hillary and Tenzing Norgay. The two men reached the top on May 29, 1953. Since then, thousands of climbers have achieved this feat and hundreds have died trying.

Every May, climbers fly into Kathmandu (kat-man-DOO), the capital city of Nepal, to begin their expeditions. Climbing parties are usually made up of about 10 climbers and 20 Sherpa guides. Sherpas are people who live on the slopes of the Himalayas and are known for their endurance at high altitudes.

Climbers first establish a base camp near the bottom of the mountain before attempting to reach the summit. For about 30 days, the climbers will move up and down between Base Camp and four higher camps, allowing their bodies to get used to the reduced amount of oxygen in the air.

To get from Base Camp to Camp 1, climbers hike across deep crevasses of ice and snow. The most dangerous part of this climb is the Khumbu Icefall. Climbers use aluminum ladders to get across it. From Camp 1, climbers travel up through a valley called the Western Cwm (coom). Here, they get their first view of the highest peaks of Everest before reaching Camp 2, or Advanced Base Camp. To reach Camp 3, travelers must trek up a sleek wall of blue glacial ice. Fixed ropes help guide the climbers as they push upward. Before climbers get to Camp 4, they must scramble over two more obstacles—the Yellow Band and the Geneva Spur, both of which require ropes to traverse them. Oxygen tanks become a necessity at Camp 4. This area is sometimes called the "death zone" because many climbers have died there.

Just before they get to the top, climbers face a final hurdle—the Hillary Step—a 40-foot wall of snow and ice. When the climbers reach the summit, most stay only minutes. They need to descend before nightfall, because temperatures can drop to –100°F (–73°C).

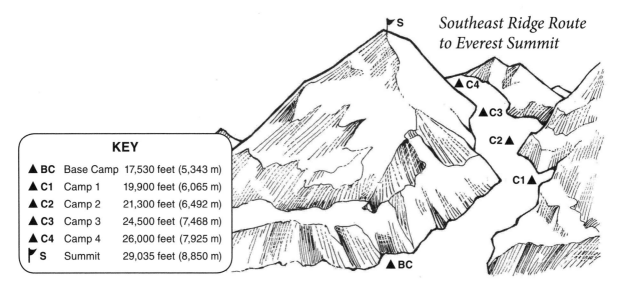

Southeast Ridge Route to Everest Summit

KEY		
▲ BC	Base Camp	17,530 feet (5,343 m)
▲ C1	Camp 1	19,900 feet (6,065 m)
▲ C2	Camp 2	21,300 feet (6,492 m)
▲ C3	Camp 3	24,500 feet (7,468 m)
▲ C4	Camp 4	26,000 feet (7,925 m)
⸕ S	Summit	29,035 feet (8,850 m)

Trek to the Summit of Everest

A. Look at the illustration and key on the other page to find out the elevation of each camp along the climb to the summit of Mount Everest. Pretend you are a climber on this expedition. Write a journal entry for each point on the route.

Base Camp: _____

_____

Camp 1: _____

_____

Camp 2: _____

_____

Camp 3: _____

_____

Camp 4: _____

_____

Summit: _____

_____

B. Would you like to climb Mount Everest? Explain why or why not.

_____

_____

_____

_____

The Indian Subcontinent

About 200 million years ago, all the continents were connected. They formed a "supercontinent" that scientists call *Pangaea*. The supercontinent was made up of plates that moved over Earth's surface at a very slow rate. Over time, the plates moved away from each other, causing the supercontinent to separate into individual landmasses. Those landmasses became the continents we know today.

One of the plates, called the Indian Plate, separated and collided with Asia 50 million years ago. The land rippled up as the two landmasses came together. The land that was pushed up became the Himalaya Mountains, with the area south of the mountains forming a large peninsula.

The continent of Asia grew bigger because of this collision. The newer part of Asia is now the region of South Asia, also known as the Indian Subcontinent. A subcontinent is a large area of land that is part of a continent, but is considered a separate geographical unit. Geographers call South Asia a subcontinent because although it is big, it is isolated from the rest of Asia due to mountain ranges.

Today the Indian Subcontinent consists of six countries. The country of India takes up three-fourths of the area. Bangladesh, Bhutan, Nepal, Sri Lanka, and parts of Pakistan make up the rest of the large peninsula.

The Indian Subcontinent

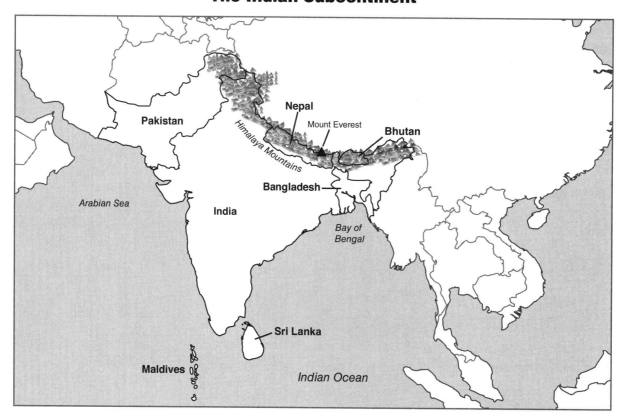

The Indian Subcontinent

Now that you have read about the Indian Subcontinent and studied the map on the other page, you are ready to complete the secret code! Read each clue and write the correct word on the numbered lines. Then use the numbers to crack the code.

1. Large bodies of _____ border the peninsula on three sides.

   $\overline{}\ \overline{}\ \overline{}\ \overline{}\ \overline{}$
   1   16   3   13   5

2. Pangaea eventually separated into the seven _____ we know today.

   $\overline{}\ \overline{}\ \overline{}\ \overline{}\ \overline{}\ \overline{}\ \overline{}\ \overline{}\ \overline{}\ \overline{}$
   15   7   8   3   10   8   13   8   3   4

3. Most _____ say that South Asia is a subcontinent.

   $\overline{}\ \overline{}\ \overline{}\ \overline{}\ \overline{}\ \overline{}\ \overline{}\ \overline{}\ \overline{}\ \overline{}\ \overline{}$
   12   13   7   12   5   16   6   11   13   5   4

4. The Indian Plate _____ with Asia 50 million years ago.

   $\overline{}\ \overline{}\ \overline{}\ \overline{}\ \overline{}\ \overline{}\ \overline{}\ \overline{}$
   15   7   9   9   10   14   13   14

5. The Indian Subcontinent is a large _____.

   $\overline{}\ \overline{}\ \overline{}\ \overline{}\ \overline{}\ \overline{}\ \overline{}\ \overline{}\ \overline{}$
   6   13   8   10   8   4   2   9   16

6. The Himalayas formed when two _____ pushed against each other.

   $\overline{}\ \overline{}\ \overline{}\ \overline{}\ \overline{}\ \overline{}$
   6   9   16   3   13   4

Crack the Code!

Some people think the Indian Subcontinent looks like an _____.

$\overline{}\ \overline{}\ \overline{}\ \overline{}\ \overline{}\ \overline{}\ \overline{}\ \overline{}\ \overline{}$
16   5   5   7   1   11   13   16   14

The Arabian and Gobi Deserts

The Arabian Desert

The Arabian Desert is the largest desert in Asia, covering most of the Arabian Peninsula in Southwest Asia. The desert has an area of about 1 million square miles (2.6 million square km). That's about one-third the size of the continental United States! Countries that lie entirely in this desert are Saudi Arabia, Kuwait, Qatar, the United Arab Emirates, Oman, and Yemen. Parts of Jordan, Syria, and Iraq also lie within the desert.

Most of the Arabian Desert is made up of barren highlands and plains. The northern part of the desert is a rocky plateau. Sand dunes are common throughout the entire desert. In fact, the southeast part of the desert contains the largest continuous area of sand on Earth.

Temperatures in the summer can reach 122°F (50°C) in this very hot, dry desert. The average winter temperature is 41°F (5°C). Most of the desert receives less than four inches (10 cm) of rainfall per year.

The Gobi Desert

The Gobi Desert is the second-largest desert in Asia and stretches across parts of southern Mongolia and northern China. The Gobi has an area of more than 500,000 square miles (1,300,000 square km).

The Gobi has rocky or sandy soil in the center, surrounded by *steppes*, or dry grasslands. Unlike the Arabian Desert, sand dunes cover only 5% of the Gobi.

The Gobi is considered a cold desert. That is because it is bitterly cold at night year-round and during the winter. In the summer, temperatures can reach as high as 113°F (45°C). But in the winter, temperatures can fall to –40°F (–40°C) at night. Most of the Gobi receives less than 10 inches (25 cm) of rainfall per year.

The Arabian and Gobi Deserts

A. Use the information and maps on the other page to complete the Venn diagram comparing the Arabian and Gobi deserts. The "Both" section has been filled in for you.

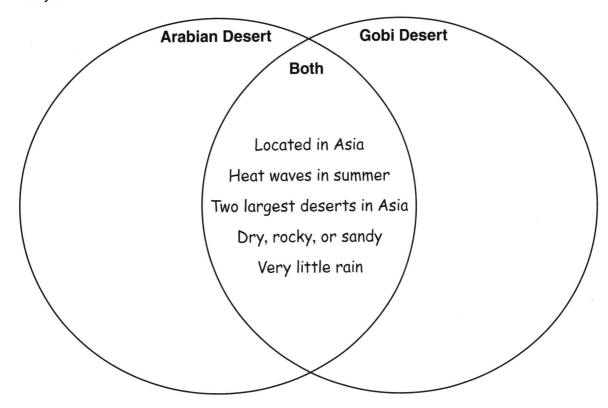

Arabian Desert   **Gobi Desert**

Both

Located in Asia

Heat waves in summer

Two largest deserts in Asia

Dry, rocky, or sandy

Very little rain

B. Use the information and maps on the other page to answer the questions.

1. Name the countries that lie entirely within the Arabian Desert.

   _____

2. Name the countries that lie partly within the Gobi Desert.

   _____

3. Which desert has the coldest winters? _____

4. Which desert receives the least amount of rainfall? _____

5. Which desert has more sand dunes? _____

Siberia's Landforms

Siberia is a huge, cold region in northern Asia. It has an area of about 4,938,000 square miles (12,789,000 square km) and lies within the country of Russia. In fact, Siberia makes up about 75% of Russia. However, less than 20% of the Russian people live there. That is because of the region's harsh, arctic climate. In much of Siberia, extreme cold temperatures, snow, and ice last for about six months of the year. The temperature in some parts can drop below –90°F (–68°C). In addition to its climate, Siberia is known for its unique landscape. The following landforms can be found in the region:

plains: large areas of flat, treeless countryside

plateaus: level areas of land that stand higher than the surrounding areas

steppes: vast, grass-covered plains rich in soil; also called *grasslands*

taiga: an evergreen forest area

tundra: an arctic area in which the top layer of soil freezes and thaws, while the second layer, called *permafrost*, stays frozen all year

uplands: elevated lands, as in hills or mountains

wetlands: a lowland area made up of marshes and swamps

A. Write the letter of the definition that matches each term. Use the information from this page to help you.

_____ 1. permafrost

_____ 2. plain

_____ 3. plateau

_____ 4. steppes

_____ 5. wetlands

_____ 6. taiga

_____ 7. tundra

_____ 8. uplands

a. a hilly area where you might find mountains

b. an arctic plain that remains frozen except for the ground just at the surface

c. grasslands that have rich soil for farming

d. an area of swampland

e. a layer of permanently frozen soil

f. a large, flat area of land

g. a cold, evergreen forest region

h. a large, mostly level area of land that stands higher than the surrounding area

Siberia's Landforms

Physical Map of Siberia

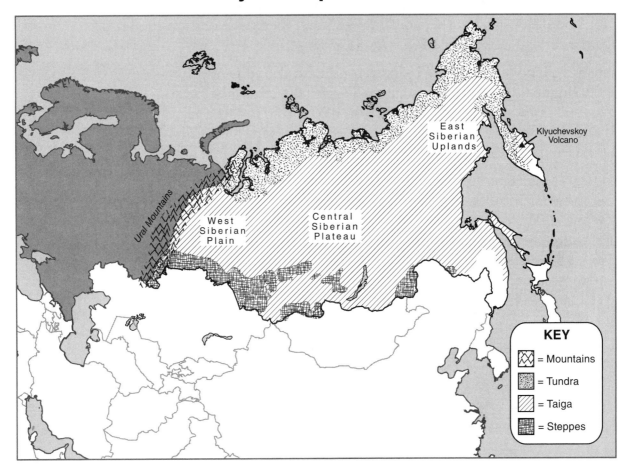

B. Write a caption for the physical map of Siberia that describes at least two of its different landforms.

_____

_____

_____

Japan's Islands

Japan is an island country that lies off the east coast of mainland Asia. Japan is made up of an *archipelago* (ark-ih-PEL-uh-go), or group of islands. It has four major islands—Hokkaido, Honshu, Kyushu, and Shikoku—and thousands of smaller ones. The islands form a curve that is about 1,200 miles (1,930 km) long.

Japan is a land of majestic, very dangerous natural landforms, including rocky peaks, deep gorges, tall waterfalls, and thick forests. Mountains and hills cover about 70% of the country. In fact, the islands are part of a great mountain range that rises from the floor of the Pacific Ocean.

Japan lies along part of the Ring of Fire, a huge area that encircles the entire Pacific Ocean where over half the world's volcanoes are found. The Japanese islands alone have more than 150 major volcanoes, and over 60 of them are active. Mount Fuji, on the island of Honshu, is the highest and most famous volcanic mountain in Japan. It is 12,388 feet (3,776 m) high.

About 1,500 earthquakes also occur in Japan each year. Most of them are minor tremors, but severe earthquakes happen every few years. Occasionally, undersea earthquakes cause a series of huge, destructive waves called *tsunamis*, which crash along Japan's Pacific coast.

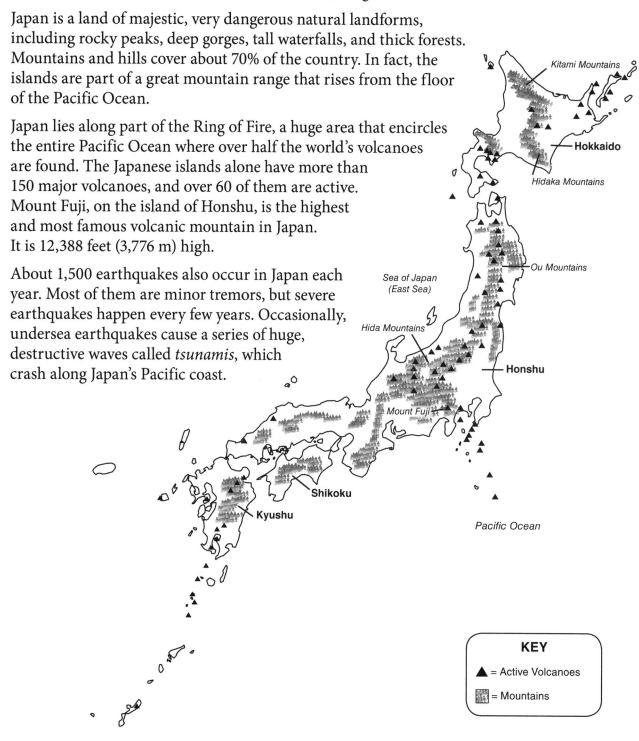

Kitami Mountains

Hokkaido

Hidaka Mountains

Ou Mountains

Sea of Japan
(East Sea)

Hida Mountains

Honshu

Mount Fuji

Shikoku

Kyushu

Pacific Ocean

KEY

▲ = Active Volcanoes

▧ = Mountains

Japan's Islands

A. Use the information on the other page to answer the questions.

1. How many major islands does Japan have?   _____

2. Which two landforms cover 70% of Japan?   _____

3. What is the name and height of the highest
   volcanic mountain in Japan?   _____

4. Of the 150 major volcanoes on Japan's islands, how   _____
   many are active?

5. What is an *archipelago?* _____

6. Describe what can happen along Japan's coast when there is a strong undersea
   earthquake.

   _____

   _____

B. Write a paragraph explaining why Japan is considered a majestic, very dangerous
place to live.

_____

_____

_____

_____

_____

_____

_____

Asia's Tropical Rainforests

In contrast to the arctic climate of the north, Southeast Asia is the continent's warm, tropical region. Rainforests grow in parts of Brunei, Cambodia, Indonesia, Laos, Malaysia, Myanmar, the Philippines, Singapore, Thailand, and Vietnam, covering about 1 million square miles (2.6 million square km) of land. The Southeast Asian rainforests are some of the most biologically diverse on the planet. However, people are destroying these rainforests faster than in any other tropical region. This is because there are few protected wildlife areas in Southeast Asia, so there is nothing to stop people from logging and farming the land.

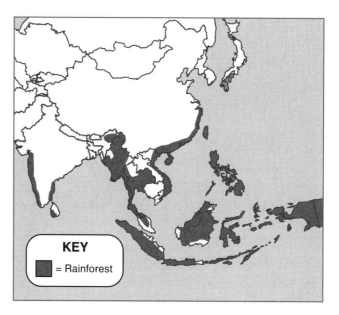

KEY

■ = Rainforest

Facts About Asian Rainforests

- The Southeast Asian rainforests are the oldest ones on Earth. They date back 70 million years.

- Winds called *monsoons* control much of the climate in the rainforests. The winds bring heavy rains and sometimes *typhoons*, or hurricanes. The rainforests receive 60 to 100 inches (152 to 254 cm) of rain each year.

- The climate is very hot and humid. Average humidity ranges from 70% to 90%. The average temperature is 80°F (27°C) in the rainforest, and the highs can reach 95°F (35°C).

- Trees grow so close together in the rainforests that falling rain often never reaches the ground.

- The *tualang* tree, a tall tree species that grows in the rainforest, can reach up to 250 feet (76 m) high. Bees build honeycombs that hang from its branches. The combs can be six feet across and contain as many as 30,000 bees.

- Two famous plants of the rainforest are pitcher plants and rafflesia. Pitcher plants are unusual because they trap and feed on insects. The rafflesia's claim to fame is that it is the world's largest flower. It is more than three feet (91 cm) wide.

- Many of the animal species that live in the rainforest, including the rhinoceros, tiger, elephant, and tapir, are on the brink of extinction.

Asia's Tropical Rainforests

A. Complete each sentence by unscrambling the word under the line.
Use the information on the other page to help you.

1. Asian rainforests are located in a _____ region.
   aciportl

2. Winds called _____ control much of the rainforest climate.
   nomsonos

3. The climate of the rainforest is hot and _____.
   mhidu

4. The _____ tree is home to thousands of bees.
   aangtul

5. The rafflesia is the world's largest _____.
   owrelf

6. _____ and Indonesia are two countries that have rainforests.
   almyasai

7. The Asian rhino, tiger, tapir, and elephant are near _____.
   citenxinot

8. The ancient rainforests of Asia have existed for 70

   _____ years.
   ilomlin

B. Write three reasons why you would or would *not* like to visit an Asian rainforest.

1. _____

   _____

2. _____

   _____

3. _____

   _____

Asia's Bodies of Water

Asia has a variety of bodies of water, from frigid arctic oceans in the north to warm tropical waters in the south. It is surrounded on three sides by the Arctic, Pacific, and Indian oceans. It is also bordered by several large seas. These include the Mediterranean and Arabian seas in the west, the South China and Philippine seas in the east, and the Bering and East Siberian seas in the north.

With a continent so big, it's no wonder there are also many large inland bodies of water, ranging from long, winding rivers to sprawling inland seas and lakes. Famous rivers include the Ganges River in India and the Yangtze (Chang Jiang) River in China. The Caspian Sea on the western border of Asia is the world's largest inland sea. In Russia, Lake Baikal is the largest freshwater lake in the world. And the Dead Sea on the border of Israel and Jordan is the lowest place on Earth.

A. Find and circle the bodies of water in the word puzzle. Words may appear across, down, or diagonally.

```
Y D P U H C J S N H E U L U C
A E H J N A R A B I A N Q I C
N F I Y S R A S V K J T F C G
G W L A B E R I N G L I H U B
T K I Z T R H Y R I C O D Q A
Z L P U G S A C D A I F U F K
E T P L W B I A P L W L Q G I
J C I J S F C S Z U W A L A S
Y I N E Y I L P A G L A K N T
R N E U T R J I Y H K F T G E
V D W C T J W A Y I G K C E M
N I R E A R S N A E N F A S U
K A V I P N N B Z Q L D A X K
D N T S N G A O L H J Q U P Y
J P A R I B A L K H A S H S O
```

Oceans:
- **Arctic**
- **Indian**
- **Pacific**

Seas:
- **Arabian**
- **Bering**
- **Caspian**
- **Philippine**

Lakes:
- **Baikal**
- **Balkhash**

Rivers:
- **Ganges**
- **Indus**
- **Yangtze**

B. Write two facts you learned about Asia's bodies of water.

1. _____

2. _____

Name _____

Asia's Bodies of Water

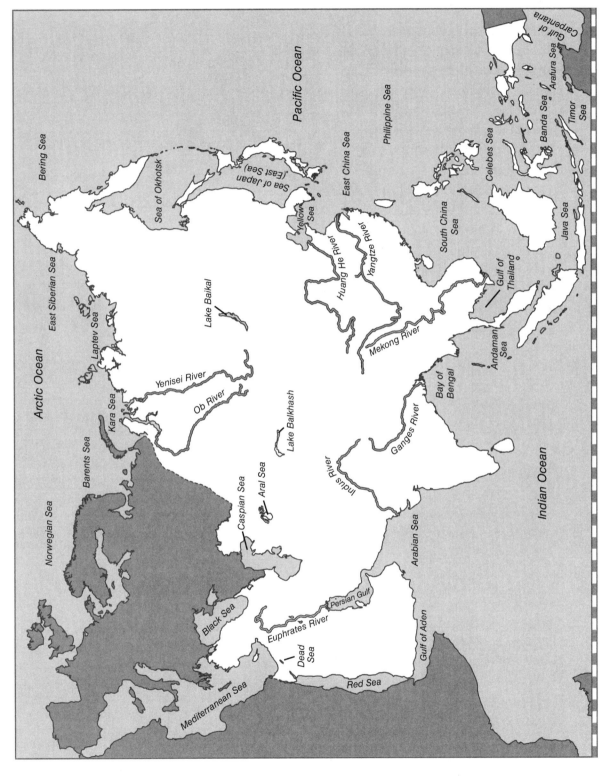

Asia's Inland Seas and Lakes

There are many types of seas in and around the continent of Asia. Some seas border the coast of the continent, such as the Sea of Okhotsk off the coast of Russia. But others are inland, completely surrounded by land. Inland seas are actually large saltwater or freshwater lakes. For example, the Dead Sea and the Sea of Galilee are both inland seas located in the Middle East. But the Dead Sea is a saltwater lake, while the Sea of Galilee is a freshwater lake. One lake, Lake Balkhash in Kazakhstan, has both fresh water and salt water.

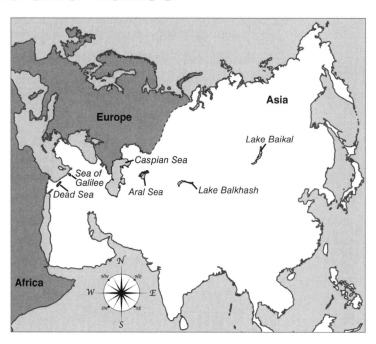

Look at the map and chart for information about some of Asia's inland seas and lakes.

Seas and Lakes	Type	Location	Interesting Facts
Aral Sea	saltwater	between Kazakhstan and Uzbekistan	It was once one of the world's largest inland bodies of water. Since the 1960s, the lake has shrunk to about a fourth of its former size due to the use of the water for farming.
Caspian Sea	saltwater	borders Russia, Kazakhstan, Azerbaijan, Iran, and Turkmenistan	It lies 92 feet (28 m) below sea level and is the world's largest inland body of water. It contains both freshwater and saltwater fish.
Dead Sea	saltwater	between Jordan and Israel	This sea lies 1,381 feet (421 m) below sea level and it is the lowest place on Earth. It is also the saltiest body of water in the world.
Lake Baikal	freshwater	Russia	This lake is the world's oldest lake, having formed about 25 million years ago. It is the deepest lake in the world and contains over 20% of the world's unfrozen fresh water.
Lake Balkhash	freshwater and saltwater	Kazakhstan	The western part of this lake has fresh water. The eastern part has salt water. Ice covers the lake from November to April.
Sea of Galilee	freshwater	Israel	This small freshwater lake in the Middle East is often mentioned in the Bible. The sea is also called *Lake Kinneret*.

Asia's Inland Seas and Lakes

A. Circle the correct body of water. Use the information on the other page to help you.

1. This sea is the world's largest inland body of water.	**Aral Sea**	**Caspian Sea**
2. This sea is the world's saltiest body of water.	**Dead Sea**	**Sea of Galilee**
3. This lake is the world's oldest lake.	**Lake Baikal**	**Lake Balkhash**
4. This lake has both fresh and salt water.	**Lake Baikal**	**Lake Balkhash**
5. This sea lies below sea level.	**Dead Sea**	**Sea of Galilee**
6. This sea is also called Lake Kinneret.	**Lake Balkhash**	**Sea of Galilee**
7. Since the 1960s, this sea has shrunk in size.	**Aral Sea**	**Dead Sea**
8. This sea is in the Middle East.	**Sea of Galilee**	**Lake Balkash**
9. This body of water contains over 20% of the world's unfrozen fresh water.	**Caspian Sea**	**Lake Baikal**
10. This sea is east of the Caspian Sea.	**Dead Sea**	**Aral Sea**

B. Use the chart on the other page to answer the questions.

1. In which country is Lake Baikal located? _____

2. Which two countries share the Aral Sea? _____

3. Which lake is entirely located in Kazakhstan? _____

4. How many countries border the Caspian Sea? _____

5. The Dead Sea and Sea of Galilee share which country? _____

Important Rivers of Asia

Asia has 32 major rivers that are over 1,000 miles (1,610 km) in length. Millions of Asians live along the valleys and deltas, or areas near the mouth of the rivers. The rivers provide irrigation for farmers. They are also important transportation routes for trade and travel.

River	Length	Interesting Facts
Euphrates (yoo-FRAY-teez)	1,700 miles (2,736 km)	The Euphrates is the longest river in Southwest Asia. The river is part of the Euphrates/Tigris river system. The world's first civilization, Mesopotamia, developed around the Euphrates and Tigris rivers.
Ganges (GAN-jeez)	1,560 miles (2,511 km)	The Ganges in India is one of the longest rivers in the world. The river plays an important part in the Hindu religion. Each year, thousands of Hindus go to the Ganges to bathe in the river and take home some of its water. Hindus believe that the water will help to purify the spirit or cure sickness.
Huang He (hwahng-HEH)	3,395 miles (5,464 km)	The Huang He is the second-longest river in China. The Huang He is sometimes called "China's Sorrow" because it floods, causing much hardship for the people who live along its banks. It is also called the *Yellow River* because it carries large amounts of soft yellow earth.
Mekong (MAY-kong)	2,600 miles (4,184 km)	The Mekong is the longest river in Southeast Asia. It has many rapids and sandbars. No other river is home to so many species of large fish. The largest is the giant carp, which is almost 5 feet (1.5 m) long. Because so many dams are being built, the populations of fish are declining.
Yangtze (yang-SEE)	3,900 miles (6,275 km)	The Yangtze is the longest river in Asia and the word's third longest. It is located in China. Chinese call the Yangtze the *Chang Jiang* or *Long River*. Thousands of people live on the Yangtze. Some live and work on wooden sailboats called *junks*. The junks are used to carry food and supplies from the country to the cities.
Yenisei (yen-uh-SAY)	2,543 miles (4,093 km)	The Yenisei is the chief river in North Asia. It is located in the Siberian region of Russia and is frozen during the winter months. Because the upper river has so many rapids, hydroelectric stations have been built to supply energy to the region. The river is also a major transport route for lumber and grain.

Important Rivers of Asia

A. Read the information in the chart on the other page. Write the name of the river to complete each sentence.

1. The _____ River is the longest river in Asia.

2. The _____ is also called the Yellow River.

3. Every year, thousands of Hindus go to the sacred _____ River.

4. The world's first civilization was built along the Tigris and

    _____ rivers.

5. Giant carp make their home in the _____ River.

6. The _____ River is 2,543 miles (4,093 km) long.

7. The _____ River is located in India.

8. The _____ River is sometimes known as "China's Sorrow."

B. Write the names of the six rivers and their lengths in order from longest to shortest. Use the chart on the other page to help you.

Rank	River	Length (in miles)
1		
2		
3		
4		
5		
6		

Review

Use words from the box to complete the crossword puzzle.

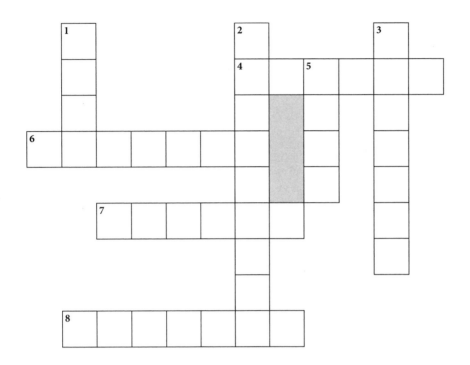

Baikal

Dead

Everest

Gobi

Himalayas

Indian

Siberia

Yangtze

Across

4. The _____ Subcontinent is a peninsula.

6. _____ is a region in Russia.

7. Lake _____ is the world's deepest lake.

8. Mount _____ is the highest peak in the world.

Down

1. The _____ Desert is a cold desert.

2. The _____ are the highest mountains in the world.

3. The _____ River is the longest in Asia.

5. The lowest place on Earth is the _____ Sea.

Valuable Resources of Asia

This section introduces students to the natural resources of Asia. Students discover that Southwest Asia is a large oil-producing region and that China is a major producer and consumer of coal energy. Students also learn about Asia's main food sources—ocean fishing and rice farming. Finally, students explore three different kinds of forests that grow in Asia and become familiar with the wild and domesticated animals that inhabit different regions of the continent.

Each skill in this section is based on the following National Geography Standards:

Essential Element 3: Physical Systems

Standard 8: The characteristics and spatial distribution of ecosystems on Earth's surface

Essential Element 5: Environment and Society

Standard 14: How human actions modify the physical environment

Standard 16: The changes that occur in the meaning, use, distribution, and importance of resources

CONTENTS

Name _____

Overview

Natural resources are the minerals, plants, animals, and other elements that humans use from their environment. Oil, coal, water, fish, fertile soil, forests, and farm animals are examples of natural resources. The continent of Asia has all these vital natural resources.

Oil and Coal

Oil is an important natural resource that is particularly plentiful in Russia and the Middle East. Countries such as Saudi Arabia, Iran, and Kuwait supply a large amount of the world's oil.

Coal is another valuable resource, with China being Asia's top producer and consumer of this burnable, carbon-based material.

Fishing and Farming

Ocean fishing is a big business in Asia. Many kinds of fish and shellfish from the Pacific and Indian oceans are staples of the Asian diet. Large fleets of fishing boats catch millions of tons of seafood each year to meet this demand.

About two-thirds of the people in Asia earn a living by farming. Rice is a major crop and a food staple for most Asian people. The fertile soil helps rice grow quickly. Asian farmers grow over 90% of the world's rice.

The Forests of Asia

Asia has three kinds of forests. The Siberian taiga is an evergreen forest in North Asia. The Northeast Asian forests are *deciduous*, or made up of trees that lose their leaves in winter. And the rainforests in Southeast Asia are made up of tropical trees.

Wild and Domesticated Animals

Asia has many unique wild animals. It is the only continent that has wild tigers. Giant pandas, orangutans, and Komodo dragons are also unique to Asia.

Animals used in farming, hauling, and other work include the Asian elephant, the water buffalo, and the dromedary camel.

Name _____

Overview

Fill in the bubble to answer each question or complete each sentence.

1. Which country is the top producer of coal?

    Ⓐ China

    Ⓑ Russia

    Ⓒ Saudi Arabia

    Ⓓ Kuwait

2. _____ is a top producer of oil.

    Ⓐ The Philippines

    Ⓑ Southeast Asia

    Ⓒ The Middle East

    Ⓓ Japan

3. Fish and _____ are staple foods for many Asian people.

    Ⓐ meat

    Ⓑ rice

    Ⓒ milk

    Ⓓ bread

4. The _____ is made up of evergreen trees.

    Ⓐ Siberian taiga

    Ⓑ Southeast Asian rainforest

    Ⓒ Northeast Asian deciduous forest

    Ⓓ none of the above

5. Which animal is used by Asian people to do work?

    Ⓐ orangutan

    Ⓑ giant panda

    Ⓒ tiger

    Ⓓ water buffalo

Oil Production in Asia

Oil is a *fossil fuel*. This means that it was formed from the remains of animals and plants that lived millions of years ago. These remains were covered by layers of soil. Over time, heat and pressure turned the remains into what is called *crude oil*.

Crude oil is a yellowish-black liquid that is usually found in underground reservoirs. A well is drilled into the reservoir to bring the crude oil to the surface. The oil is then sent to a refinery, or factory, where it is separated into usable products such as gasoline, diesel fuel, and heating oil.

Crude oil is often called "black gold" because it is so valuable. It provides much of the world's fuel supply, it's expensive to produce, and it takes so long to form that there is only a limited supply of it on Earth. Production of crude oil is an important industry in the Middle East, where huge reservoirs lie beneath Saudi Arabia, Iran, and several other Middle Eastern countries. However, the single largest oil-producing country in all of Asia is Russia.

Asia's Top Oil-Producing Countries
one barrel = 42 gallons (159 liters)

Rank	Country	Region	Barrels Produced a Day
1	Russia	North Asia	9,980,000
2	Saudi Arabia	Middle East	9,200,000
3	Iran	Middle East	4,700,000
4	China	East Asia	3,725,000
5	United Arab Emirates (UAE)	Middle East	2,948,000
6	Kuwait	Middle East	2,613,000
7	Iraq	Middle East	2,420,000
8	Kazakhstan	Central Asia	1,445,000
9	Qatar	Middle East	1,125,000
10	Azerbaijan	Southwest Asia	1,099,000

2009 statistics from Energy Information Administration

Oil Production in Asia

A. Read each statement. Circle **yes** if it is true or **no** if it is false. Use the information on the other page to help you.

1. Crude oil is called "black gold" because it has gold in it.   **Yes**   **No**

2. Russia produces less than 9,000,000 barrels of oil per day.   **Yes**   **No**

3. Saudi Arabia is the top oil producer in the Middle East.   **Yes**   **No**

4. Kazakhstan is the only Central Asian country that produces oil.   **Yes**   **No**

5. China ranks third and Iran ranks fourth in oil production.   **Yes**   **No**

6. The country that produces the most oil per day is in North Asia.   **Yes**   **No**

7. Kuwait produces more oil per day than the UAE.   **Yes**   **No**

8. Ninth-ranked Qatar produces 1,125,000 barrels of oil per day.   **Yes**   **No**

9. The Middle East has six of the top 10 oil-producing countries.   **Yes**   **No**

10. Earth's supply of crude oil is unlimited.   **Yes**   **No**

B. Russia produces close to 10,000,000 barrels of oil per day. One barrel equals 42 gallons, or 159 liters. Use your math skills to answer the questions. Circle the correct answer.

1. About how many gallons of oil does Russia produce per day?

   4,200 gallons   **420,000,000 gallons**   **42,000,000 gallons**

2. About how many liters of oil does Russia produce per day?

   159,000 liters   **15,900,000 liters**   **1,590,000,000 liters**

3. How does a gallon of oil compare to a liter?

   **a gallon is about four times   a liter is about four times
   larger than a liter   larger than a gallon**

China's Coal Energy

Like oil, coal is a fossil fuel, but it is a solid black or brown rock that formed from decaying plant matter that has been pressed together for millions of years. Because this process takes so long, Earth has a limited supply of coal.

The main use of coal is in the production of electric power. Coal is made mostly of carbon, which can be easily lit and burned. This produces energy in the form of heat. The heat from the burning coal makes steam that drives the engines in electric power plants.

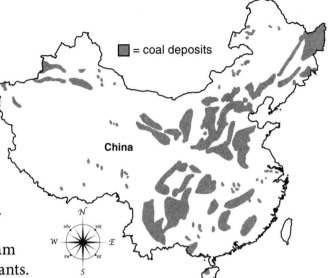

= coal deposits

China

China is the world's largest producer of coal. Many parts of China have coal deposits, but the most productive coal fields are located in the north. Coal is mined, or dug up, from deep inside Earth. China has about 25,000 working coal mines.

China is also the world's largest consumer of coal, meaning it uses the most coal. The country is dependent on coal for fuel. About 70% of China's electrical energy comes from coal-burning plants.

China's Coal Production and Use*

1980–2020

Year	Amount Produced (tons)	Amount Consumed (tons)
1980	684 hundred million	678 hundred million
1990	1 billion, 200 hundred million	1 billion, 100 hundred million
2000	1 billion, 300 hundred million	1 billion, 300 hundred million
2010	3 billion, 1 hundred million	1 billion, 700 hundred million
2020 projections	4 billion, 900 hundred million	2 billion, 400 hundred million

*Figures have been rounded to the nearest hundred million.

Energy Information Administration, International Figures

China's Coal Energy

A. Complete each sentence by unscrambling the word under the line. Use the information on the other page to help you.

1. Coal is a natural _____.
   ecurosre

2. China is the world's largest _____ of coal.
   cudorpre

3. Most of China's electric _____ comes from coal.
   genyer

4. In 2000, China produced and _____ about the same
   amount of coal. **mesunocd**

5. By 2020, almost five _____ tons of coal are expected
   to be produced in China. **ibolnil**

6. According to the chart, China produced a much _____
   amount of coal in 2010 than it consumed. **gralre**

7. The heat from burning coal is used to produce _____.
   yeclritiect

8. Because coal is a form of _____, it can be easily burned.
   robcan

B. Use the map and information on the other page to answer the questions.

1. Where are there more coal deposits in China, _____
   in the east or west?

2. About how many coal mines does China have? _____

3. Which part of China has the most productive _____
   coal fields?

Fishing in Asia

On a continent surrounded by oceans, it's no surprise that fish, shellfish, and seaweed make up a large part of Asia's food supply. The countries that distribute the most of these three staples are China, Japan, Russia, Indonesia, and Thailand.

Commercial Fishing

Fish provides the main source of protein in the diets of millions of Asians. The Asian diet also includes shellfish such as crabs, clams, lobsters, mussels, octopuses, oysters, and shrimp. To meet this need, the Asian fishing industry employs about 30 million fishermen.

Large commercial fishing vessels catch millions of tons of fish and shellfish each year. Japan alone brought in more than 4 million tons in 2007.

Fishermen use large nets that are miles long to catch big fish such as tuna. Shellfish are caught in baskets, boxes, and other traps that are dropped into the sea.

Harvesting seaweed is also a big business. Seaweed is used not only in foods, especially in Japan, but in many medicines and beauty products.

Traditional Fishing

Not all fishing is done by large fishing vessels. Small boats are used near the coastlines. Traditional fishermen in Southeast Asia also depend on river fishing to provide food for their families. For example, on the Mekong River in Vietnam, Vietnamese fishermen take their catch to market in a riverboat called a *sampan*.

Fish Markets

Asia is famous for its large fish markets. The largest fish market in the world, the Tsukiji Market, is in Tokyo, Japan. Here, over 400 different types of seafood are sold. Every day there is an auction to sell gigantic tuna to markets around the world.

There are also floating markets in Asia. Hundreds of workers, mostly women, pile local produce and fish into their flat-bottom boats. They float through canals on the Chao Phraya River in Bangkok, Thailand, selling their goods to families that live along the river.

Fishing in Asia

A. Find and circle the words in the word puzzle. Words may appear across, down, or diagonally.

```
A F B F I S D E E J R C B A Q
B I W H S H R I M P W H K T P
M S G C H N E J L O C Z J L P
C H A L E M S A M P A N S Y I
D E I Z L V A G M E O B E X O
A R W O L H B V M C T Y A H X
U M B S F L E E T I H H W B U
O E I N I M Z I J T P S E T R
P N G A S F I B E U W I E G C
A I X L H K U K L N O I D Z E
X S F V T K R E L S L F E H O
P D C B W A Y F I S E K R V C
R A N W M X C O K P O N V H E
Y A T E V T U N A Z C O R S A
M V E H Z E G U L N U M X A N
```

fishermen
fleet
market
ocean
sampan
seaweed
shellfish
shrimp
tuna

B. Write a sentence that gives facts about fishing in Asia. Use at least three words from the word box.

_____

_____

_____

_____

Rice: An Asian Staple

Fast Facts About Rice

- Rice is a cereal grain. It is the chief crop of Asia.

- Asian farmers grow over 90% of the world's rice.

- More than half the world's population depends on rice as a food staple.

- There are about 250 million rice farms in Asia. Together they produce more than 575 million tons of rice per year.

- In some Asian languages, the word for *eat* and *eat rice* is the same.

- Rice farming in Southeast Asia dates back to about 5,000 BC.

- Today in Southeast Asia, planting and harvesting rice is often done without machinery. Some farmers use oxen or water buffalo to pull hand plows.

- Most rice grows in areas of the world with a yearly rainfall of at least 40 inches (100 cm).

- Rice requires an average temperature of at least 70°F (21°C) throughout its growing season in order to grow properly.

- Rice grows best in a field covered with shallow water. Asian farmers build low dirt walls called *levees* to hold water in their *paddies*, or fields.

World's Top Rice-Growing Countries

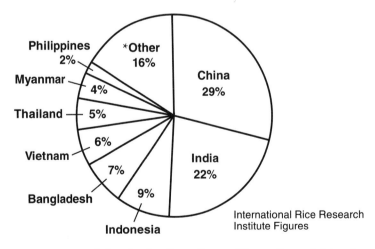

Philippines 2%
*Other 16%
China 29%
Myanmar 4%
Thailand 5%
Vietnam 6%
India 22%
Bangladesh 7%
9%
Indonesia

International Rice Research Institute Figures

* The Asian countries of Cambodia, Iran, Japan, Korea, Laos, Malaysia, Pakistan, and Sri Lanka also grow rice. Each of these eight countries grows about 1% of the world's rice, or 8% of the total, while countries from other continents make up the remaining 8%.

A. Color each section of the circle graph a different color.

Rice: An Asian Staple

B. Use the fast facts and the graph on the other page to complete the code. Read each clue below to find each answer. Then use the numbers to crack the code!

1. Rice is called a cereal ____.

 $\overline{9}$ $\overline{4}$ $\overline{14}$ $\overline{8}$ $\overline{6}$

2. Asian farmers grow over 90 ____ of the world's rice.

 $\overline{5}$ $\overline{11}$ $\overline{4}$ $\overline{13}$ $\overline{11}$ $\overline{6}$ $\overline{2}$

3. Most Asian rice fields are called ____.

 $\overline{5}$ $\overline{14}$ $\overline{12}$ $\overline{12}$ $\overline{8}$ $\overline{11}$ $\overline{3}$

4. Asian farmers depend on warm temperatures and plenty of ____ to grow rice.

 $\overline{4}$ $\overline{14}$ $\overline{8}$ $\overline{6}$ $\overline{10}$ $\overline{14}$ $\overline{7}$ $\overline{7}$

5. China and ____ are the world's top producers of rice.

 $\overline{8}$ $\overline{6}$ $\overline{12}$ $\overline{8}$ $\overline{14}$

6. Rice fields are covered with ____.

 $\overline{15}$ $\overline{14}$ $\overline{2}$ $\overline{11}$ $\overline{4}$

Crack the Code!

This grass, called ____, is native to North America and is not actually rice.

 $\overline{15}$ $\overline{8}$ $\overline{7}$ $\overline{12}$ $\overline{4}$ $\overline{8}$ $\overline{13}$ $\overline{11}$

Asia's Forests

Forests are critical to the health of our planet.
They provide homes for millions of plants
and animals, and they help regulate the
oxygen in the atmosphere. The forests of
Asia also provide their own unique
resources for the people who live there.
Three important kinds of forests are
found in Asia.

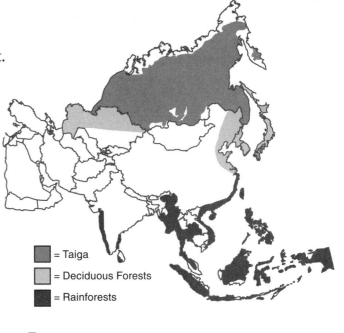

= Taiga

= Deciduous Forests

= Rainforests

North Asia's Taiga

Taiga is the Russian word for "forest."
The Siberian taiga is the largest forest
in the world. *Coniferous*, or evergreen,
trees grow in the taiga. They have long,
waxy needles that stay on the trees in winter. Evergreens
in the taiga, including cedar, pine, spruce, and fir trees,
have thin trunks and grow close together. Animals such
as the brown bear, moose, wolf, red fox, and reindeer make
their home in the taiga. Large areas of the forest are
harvested for lumber and paper products.

Northeast Asia's Deciduous Forests

A deciduous forest is made up of trees that lose their leaves in winter. The Northeast
Asian deciduous forests cover parts of Korea, China, Russia, and Japan. Common
deciduous trees in this area include the elm, walnut, oak,
and birch. The precious Asian ginseng root is also found in
the forests of Northeast Asia. Asian ginseng is a gnarled
root used for medicinal purposes not only in Asia, but
throughout the world.

Southeast Asia's Rainforests

Rainforests cover about one million square miles (2.6 million square km) of Southeast
Asia. The rainforests are in India and extend eastward through Vietnam and
southeast China. Rainforests are also on the islands of Indonesia, Malaysia, and the
Philippines. A single family of trees called the *dipterocarps* forms the rainforest
canopy. The trees can reach heights of 120 feet (37 m). But the tallest tree
in Southeast Asia's rainforests, and the third-tallest tree species
in the world, is the tualang tree. It can reach heights of up to
280 feet (85 m). Large honeybees make giant honeycombs in
these trees, and the honey is harvested by locals.

Asia's Forests

A. Write the letter of the definition that matches each forest term.

_____ 1. coniferous trees

_____ 2. deciduous trees

_____ 3. dipterocarp

_____ 4. ginseng

_____ 5. North Asia

_____ 6. Northeast Asia

_____ 7. rainforest

_____ 8. Southeast Asia

_____ 9. taiga

_____ 10. tualang tree

a. a Russian word for *forest*

b. a dense tropical forest where a lot of rain falls

c. a region known for its coniferous forests

d. the third-tallest tree species in the world

e. a region known for its rainforests

f. another word for *evergreen trees*

g. a family of trees that form the canopy of a rainforest

h. a gnarled root used for medicinal purposes

i. trees that lose their leaves in winter

j. an area known for its deciduous forests

B. Write one important fact that you learned about each type of Asian forest. Use complete sentences.

North Asia's taiga: _____

_____

Northeast Asia's deciduous forests: _____

_____

Southeast Asia's rainforests: _____

_____

Amazing Wildlife of Asia

Giant Panda	Orangutan

The Chinese call their beloved panda a "large bear-cat."

In the Malay language, "orangutan" means "man of the forest."

Habitat
- mountain regions in central China
- lives in cool, wet bamboo forests

Habitat
- rainforests of Southeast Asia
- lives high in the treetops

Characteristics
- black and white bear
- weighs up to 300 lbs (136 kg)
- poor vision, but keen sense of smell

Characteristics
- large, reddish-brown ape
- weighs up to 220 lbs (100 kg)
- human-like thumbs for grasping

Diet
- eats 28 lbs (12.5 kg) of bamboo a day
- spends 12 hours a day eating

Diet
- figs, nuts, leaves, bark, insects
- gets rainwater from leaves and off its own hair

Reproduction
- female gives birth to one or two cubs after a five-month pregnancy
- newborn cubs weigh 5 ounces (142 g)

Reproduction
- female gives birth to one baby after a nine-month pregnancy
- newborn baby weighs 3 to 4 lbs (1 to 2 kg)

Behavior
- shy, solitary animal
- skilled tree-climber and good swimmer

Behavior
- swings from trees, walks on four limbs
- baby clings to mother while she travels
- male roars when threatened

Enemies
- snow leopards, wild dogs
- eagles hunt panda cubs

Enemies
- no natural predators

Status
- endangered species

Status
- endangered species

Amazing Wildlife of Asia

Komodo Dragon

People in Indonesia call the Komodo dragon the "land crocodile."

Habitat
- four small islands in Indonesia
- lives in dry forests and savannas

Characteristics
- largest lizard in the world
- weighs 300 lbs (136 kg)
- sharp claws and muscular tail
- keen eyesight and sense of smell

Diet
- carrion (dead animals), deer, goats, pigs
- has been known to kill humans
- can consume 80% of its own body weight in a single meal

Reproduction
- female lays 15 to 30 eggs
- hatchlings weigh less than 4 ounces (100 g) and are 16 inches (40 cm) long

Behavior
- solitary, territorial lizard
- can climb trees and swim

Enemies
- no natural enemies

Status
- endangered species

King Cobra

The scientific name for the king cobra means "snake eater."

Habitat
- rainforests and plains of India, southern China, Southeast Asia

Characteristics
- longest venomous snake in the world
- olive-green, tan, or black coloring with yellow crossbands

Diet
- other snakes, including venomous snakes
- lizards, frogs, small mammals
- swallows prey whole

Reproduction
- female lays 18 to 50 eggs
- young hatch in about 70 days
- the only snake that builds nests to lay eggs

Behavior
- when threatened, raises its head off the ground and spreads its neck into a hood

Enemies
- mongoose, birds of prey such as owls and eagles

Status
- numbers declining due to loss of habitat

Amazing Wildlife of Asia

| Rhinoceros Hornbill | Birdwing Butterfly |

Ancient people worshipped this bird as a god of war.

This butterfly's official name is the Queen Alexandra's Birdwing butterfly.

Habitat
- rainforests of Malaysia, Indonesia, Borneo, Java, Sumatra

Habitat
- small strip of lowland coastal rainforest in New Guinea

Characteristics
- large black bird with white belly
- has a bony orange and red casque (horn) protruding from its head
- long beak and thick, curly eyelashes

Characteristics
- largest butterfly in the world
- wingspan up to 1 foot (30 cm)
- female has brown wings, tan body
- male has blue and green markings with a bright yellow body
- poisonous if eaten

Diet
- fruits, insects, small animals

Diet
- sips nectar from the toxic pipevine plant, using its tube-like "tongue"

Reproduction
- female lays one to two eggs
- birds use mud to seal female inside a tree cavity to lay her eggs
- eggs hatch in 30 days; female breaks out of cavity and reseals chicks inside for 80 days

Reproduction
- female lays eggs on plants
- black and red caterpillars hatch from eggs; turn into pupa
- adult butterflies emerge

Behavior
- lives with mate
- makes a honking, squawking sound

Behavior
- males chase off rivals, including birds

Enemies
- monkeys, snakes

Enemies
- few, due to poisonous nature

Status
- threatened species

Status
- very rare and endangered species

Amazing Wildlife of Asia

A. Read each statement and circle the animal that is described. Use the information on the other pages to help you.

1. This animal has no natural predators.   **Rhinoceros Hornbill**   **Orangutan**

2. China is home to this shy animal.   **Birdwing Butterfly**   **Giant Panda**

3. This animal is the world's largest lizard.   **King Cobra**   **Komodo Dragon**

4. A casque tops the head of this animal.   **Rhinoceros Hornbill**   **King Cobra**

5. When threatened, this animal stretches its neck into the shape of a hood.   **King Cobra**   **Komodo Dragon**

6. This animal is rare and poisonous.   **Birdwing Butterfly**   **Orangutan**

7. This animal feeds on bamboo 12 hours a day.   **Rhinoceros Hornbill**   **Giant Panda**

8. This animal eats venomous snakes.   **King Cobra**   **Orangutan**

9. The young of this animal clings to its mother while she travels.   **Orangutan**   **Giant Panda**

10. The female of this animal lays her eggs in a sealed tree cavity.   **Rhinoceros Hornbill**   **Komodo Dragon**

B. Which of the six animals described on the other pages is your favorite? Write three reasons why.

_____

_____

_____

Tigers of Asia

Tigers are the largest members of the cat family. They can only be found in Asia. However, over the last 100 years, hunting and forest destruction have reduced tiger populations. Scientists think only about 3,200 of these endangered animals still survive in the wild today.

At one time, eight different subspecies of tigers lived in Asia, but three became extinct in the 1900s. The five remaining subspecies are the Bengal, Indo-Chinese, Sumatran, Siberian, and South China tigers. The Bengal tiger lives in the forests of India. The Indo-Chinese tiger lives in the forests of China, Thailand, and Myanmar. The Sumatran tiger lives on the island of Sumatra in Indonesia. The Siberian tiger lives in the forests between Russia and China. And the South China tiger lives only in south-central China. They are the most endangered tigers in the world. There may be only 20 to 24 of them left in the wild.

Fast Facts About Tigers

- Most adult male tigers weigh about 400 pounds (180 kg). They are about 9 feet (3 m) long, including a 3 foot (1 m) tail. Females are smaller in size and weight.

- The tiger's coat ranges from brownish-yellow to orange-red and is marked by black stripes. Each tiger has a unique stripe pattern. Most tigers have yellow eyes.

- A few tigers have white coats with brown stripes and blue eyes. White tigers are extremely rare. There are about 100 white tigers and they all live in zoos.

- An adult male tiger lives alone and is very aggressive. It marks a large territory with its scent to keep other tigers away.

- A female tiger, called a *tigress*, has one to six cubs. Newborn cubs weigh only about 2 pounds (1 kg).

- Female cubs settle down in a territory near their mother. Males tend to roam far from their birthplace.

- Tigers hunt deer, antelope, wild cattle, and wild pigs. Some may even attack young rhinos and elephants.

- A hungry tiger can eat as much as 60 lbs (27 kg) of meat in one night.

- A tiger's roar can be heard as far as 2 miles (3 km) away.

- Tigers are good swimmers. They can swim across rivers and from island to island.

Tigers of Asia

A. Use the key below to color the picture of the Bengal tiger.

> **KEY**
>
> **White:** belly, muzzle (area around mouth), chin, and beard
> **Orange-brown:** nose, face, ears, tail, paws, and rest of body

B. Write a paragraph about tigers that includes at least three facts. Use the information on the other page to help you.

_____

_____

_____

_____

_____

Working Animals

Many Asian people use *domesticated*, or tamed, animals to do work. The animals are commonly called "beasts of burden" because they carry heavy loads.

The Arabian Camel

The Arabian camel is a *dromedary*, which is a camel that has one hump. The hump can store up to 80 pounds (36 kg) of fat and allows a camel to travel up to 100 desert miles (161 km) without water. An Arabian camel stands 7 feet (2 m) tall at the hump and can weigh up to 1,600 pounds (726 kg).

Arabian camels have been domesticated for almost 3,500 years. They are used mostly as pack animals, meaning they carry large loads. In fact, they can carry up to 200 pounds (90 kg) while walking 25 miles (40 km) a day through the hot, sandy desert. Carrying people and their goods through the vast deserts of Southwest Asia has earned this camel the nickname "ship of the desert."

The Asian Elephant

An Asian elephant is similar to an African elephant, but has differently shaped ears and is smaller. Still, the animal can weigh up to 11,500 pounds (5,216 kg). The shoulder height of the Asian elephant is 9 feet (3 m). Its trunk is a long nose that can grab objects. The tusks are used to dig for roots and water and to strip bark from trees.

For more than 2,000 years, people have domesticated Asian elephants. They are used mostly for transportation and in the forestry business of South and Southeast Asia. The elephants work in rugged country, hauling cut trees out of forests. Rangers also ride on elephants' backs, patrolling protected areas. Unfortunately, Asian elephants are endangered. Conservationists are working to save these majestic beasts.

The Water Buffalo

The water buffalo is a large type of cattle. The bulls, or males, are 6 feet (2 m) tall and can weigh from 1,500 to 2,650 pounds (680 to 1,202 kg). Their horns can measure 12 feet (4 m) from tip to tip.

Water buffalo have been domesticated for more than 5,000 years. There are about 153 million domesticated water buffalo in South and Southeast Asia. They are used mostly for plowing and transportation. The water buffalo, in fact, has made rice farming possible on a large scale because of its ability to plow knee-deep in mud. No wonder this giant beast is called the "living tractor of the East."

Working Animals

A. Write a definition for each of the following terms, using the information on the other page.

domesticated: _____

dromedary: _____

pack animal: _____

B. Use the information on the other page to answer the questions.

1. What do people mean when they say camels are the "ships of the desert"?

   _____

2. Why do people call water buffalo the "living tractors of the East"?

   _____

C. Draw a picture of an Arabian camel, Asian elephant, or water buffalo. Write a caption next to the picture. Use the information and pictures on the other page to help you.

Review

Use words from the box to complete the crossword puzzle.

buffalo

dragon

fishing

forest

orangutan

resources

rice

tigers

Across

1. Asians use water ____ as work animals.

5. Asian farmers grow over 90% of the world's ____.

6. ____ means "man of the forest."

8. The Siberian taiga is the largest ____ in the world.

Down

2. Commercial ocean ____ is a major industry.

3. The Komodo ____ is the largest lizard in the world.

4. Oil and coal are natural ____.

7. ____ are only found in Asia.

The 7 Continents: Asia • EMC 3734 • © Evan-Moor Corp.

Asian Culture

This section introduces students to the architecture, education, arts, beliefs, and traditions of Asia. Students compare different types of Asian cuisine, learn about the six major religions of Asia, and study the traditions of Chinese New Year and the Japanese Doll Festival. They also discover four major tourist attractions in Asia.

Each skill in this section is based on the following National Geography Standards:

Essential Element 2: Places and Regions

Standard 6: How culture and experience influence people's perceptions of places and regions

Essential Element 4: Human Systems

Standard 10: The characteristics, distribution, and complexity of Earth's cultural mosaics

CONTENTS

Overview

The *culture* of a group of people consists of their beliefs, customs, and traditions. Culture is displayed in people's artwork, literature, language, architecture, and cuisine. The rich diversity of Asia's many different cultures reflects the vastness of the continent.

Tourist Attractions

Many world-famous historic and cultural tourist attractions are found in Asia, including the Taj Mahal in India, the ancient city of Petra in Jordan, the Great Wall of China, and Angkor Wat in Cambodia.

Arts and Entertainment

Asia has a booming arts and entertainment community. Mumbai, India, is the home of Bollywood, the world's largest film industry. In China, music, dance, and martial arts are performed at the famous Beijing Opera. Japanese manga, a form of comics that are story-driven, is popular not only in Japan, but in the United States and Europe.

Major Religions of Asia

Daily life in Asia is greatly influenced by the religious beliefs of its people. Six major religions—Buddhism, Christianity, Confucianism, Hinduism, Islam, and Judaism—were founded in Asia. Christianity, Islam, and Judaism began in the Middle East. Confucianism began in China, and Buddhism and Hinduism originated in India.

Education in Asia

In Asia, getting a good education is very important. Although there are many rural areas that do not have access to schools or textbooks, education is stressed in most cities. Japan has one of the top education systems in the world. Elementary school students go to school 240 days of the year. For older students, India has some of the best universities, colleges, and technical institutes on the continent.

Asian Cuisine

Popular foods such as sushi, curry, and pad Thai noodles originated in Asia. The diverse foods of Asia have influenced cooking all over the world.

Celebrations

Every country in Asia has its own special holidays and celebrations. Two of the most popular are Chinese New Year, which begins on the first new moon between January and February, and Japan's Doll Festival, or Hina Matsuri, a day of prayer for the health and happiness of young girls.

Name _____

Overview

Fill in the bubble to answer each question or complete each sentence.

1. Hina Matsuri is a festival held in ____.

   Ⓐ China

   Ⓑ India

   Ⓒ Japan

   Ⓓ Cambodia

2. Which of these is *not* a major religion of Asia?

   Ⓐ Islam

   Ⓑ Hina Matsuri

   Ⓒ Buddhism

   Ⓓ Hinduism

3. Which statement about education was made in the passage?

   Ⓐ There are no universities in India.

   Ⓑ Japan has one of the worst education systems on the continent.

   Ⓒ Students go to school 240 days of the year in Japan.

   Ⓓ Japan has the best universities in the world.

4. Which major tourist attraction is located in China?

   Ⓐ the Great Wall

   Ⓑ Petra

   Ⓒ the Taj Mahal

   Ⓓ Angkor Wat

5. Which statement is true about the culture of Asia?

   Ⓐ The culture of all Asian people is the same.

   Ⓑ Artwork, literature, and cuisine are not parts of Asian culture.

   Ⓒ Religion is the best part of Asian culture.

   Ⓓ Asian culture is very diverse.

Tourist Attractions

Asia is a continent filled with breathtaking cultural and historic sites that draw millions of tourists each year. From amazing architecture to ancient places of wonder, Asia contains several world-famous tourist attractions.

Taj Mahal

The majestic Taj Mahal in India is a mausoleum, a type of tomb. It was built by Emperor Shah Jahan in memory of his wife, Mumtaz Mahal, who died in 1631. The Taj Mahal took 20,000 workers and 22 years to complete. Its famous dome is made of white marble and is surrounded by a 980 square foot (300 square meter) garden with pools that reflect the building's image.

Taj Mahal

Petra

Petra is an ancient city carved into the mountains of Jordan. It was an important stop on the spice trade route and had a population of about 20,000 residents. Although most of the city's homes were destroyed in earthquakes over time, many of its rock-carved buildings still survive, including theaters and temples. Petra was even featured in the 1989 film *Indiana Jones and the Last Crusade*.

a building in Petra

The Great Wall of China

When the Great Wall was first built more than 2,000 years ago, it was a series of separate walls constructed by different states. The Great Wall as we know it today was completed during the Ming Dynasty (AD 1368–1644) and stretches 5,500 miles (8,850 km) through China.

Great Wall of China

Angkor Wat

Built in the 12th century in Cambodia, Angkor Wat was built as a Hindu temple and later became a Buddhist temple. Every year, it draws hundreds of thousands of tourists, who marvel at its architecture and the elaborate religious and historical scenes that decorate its walls. The temple is so famous that its image is featured on the Cambodian flag.

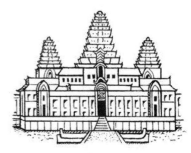

Angkor Wat

Tourist Attractions

A. Use the information on the other page to help you answer the questions.

1. In approximately what year was the Taj Mahal completed?

    _____

2. What architectural feature makes the ancient city of Petra unique?

    _____

3. How long is the Great Wall of China?

    _____

4. Which attraction is featured on the Cambodian flag?

    _____

5. Which place was featured in the movie *Indiana Jones and the Last Crusade*?

    _____

6. Why did Emperor Shah Jahan build the Taj Mahal?

    _____

7. What kind of temple was Angkor Wat originally?

    _____

8. About how long ago was the Great Wall first built?

    _____

B. Which tourist attraction would you most like to visit? Explain your answer.

_____

_____

Arts and Entertainment

Art is more than just drawing or painting. It can be any kind of creative expression, such as dance, literature, music, and theater. All of these art forms, and many others, flourish in Asia. Asian art, in fact, has inspired artists and performers across the globe, and its influence can be seen in American movies, TV shows, fashion, and more.

Bollywood

The largest film industry in the world is not Hollywood in the United States. It's Bollywood, based in Mumbai, India. The name *Bollywood* is a cross of *Bombay* (the former name of the city of Mumbai) and *Hollywood*. More than 700 films are produced in Bollywood each year, most of them musicals. Each movie features elaborate song-and-dance routines, with colorful costumes and sets. Actors lip-sync the words to prerecorded songs performed by professional singers. The dances are a combination of classical Indian and folk dance with modern Western styles.

Japanese Manga

Manga, a type of comics, is extremely popular in Japan. The Japanese word *manga* means "whimsical pictures." The comics feature black-and-white drawings of often fantastical characters. Manga drawings are accompanied by long stories that focus on the characters' struggles. The comics can sometimes run as long as 400 pages! Manga is not just for kids. There are categories of Manga for teens and adults, as well as manga geared specifically to girls. Many animated movies and TV shows are based on manga comics.

The Beijing Opera

The Beijing Opera is one of China's national treasures. Performed at the Liyuan Theatre, this spectacular cultural event involves actors and singers wearing colorful costumes and elaborate makeup. Acrobats, jesters, and storytellers present dramatic plays with singing, dancing, and martial arts. The productions are based on legendary tales of historic events.

performers of the Beijing Opera

Arts and Entertainment

A. Read each statement. Circle **yes** if it is true or **no** if it is false.

1. Martial arts can be a part of a Beijing Opera performance.　　Yes　　No

2. Manga is a type of Japanese comics.　　Yes　　No

3. Manga stories are quite short.　　Yes　　No

4. In Bollywood films, actors sing their own songs.　　Yes　　No

5. Beijing Opera productions are based on historic events.　　Yes　　No

6. For something to be considered art, it must be drawn or painted.　　Yes　　No

7. The name *Bollywood* is a combination of *Hollywood* and the former name for *Mumbai*.　　Yes　　No

8. Colorful costumes are a feature of both the Beijing Opera and Bollywood movies.　　Yes　　No

9. Manga artists draw mostly ordinary characters.　　Yes　　No

10. Bollywood movies are mostly musicals.　　Yes　　No

11. The Liyuan Theatre is in Japan.　　Yes　　No

12. Manga comics are brightly colored.　　Yes　　No

B. Which would you most like to do—go to the Beijing Opera, see a Bollywood movie, or read a manga comic book? Why?

_____

_____

_____

Major Religions of Asia

Most of the world's major religions began in Asia. Buddhism and Hinduism were founded in India, and Confucianism developed in China. Christianity, Islam, and Judaism all came from the Middle East region of Asia. Christianity and Judaism began in the area that is now Israel, while Islam started in what is now called Saudi Arabia.

Daily life in Asia is strongly influenced by people's religious beliefs.

The Dharma Wheel symbolizes Buddha's teachings of the path to enlightenment.

The cross is a symbol that reminds Christians that Jesus died on the cross.

Buddhism

Origin: India, 2,500 years ago

Leader: Siddhartha Gautama, known as Buddha, the Enlightened One

Teachings: Followers devote their lives to finding release from suffering. They try to live a balanced life without extremes. The ultimate goal is to reach a state of peace and happiness called *nirvana*.

Sacred Book: the Tripitaka

Places of Worship: temples and homes

Major Festival: Wesak, the celebration of Buddha's life

Followers: 300 million worldwide

Asian Countries Where Practiced Most: Cambodia, Laos, Mongolia, Myanmar, North Korea, Singapore, Sri Lanka, Thailand, and Vietnam

Christianity

Origin: Israel, 2,000 years ago

Leader: Jesus of Nazareth, known as Jesus Christ, the Annointed One

Teachings: Followers believe in one God. They believe that God sent Jesus to save all people from sin, and that people who believe in God and show love and forgiveness will go to heaven.

Sacred Book: the Bible

Places of Worship: churches, chapels, and cathedrals

Major Festivals: Christmas and Easter

Followers: 2.2 billion worldwide

Asian Countries Where Practiced Most: Armenia, Cyprus, Georgia, Lebanon, the Philippines, and Russia; spreading quickly in China

Major Religions of Asia

The Chinese character for water represents the religion of Confucianism.

The star and crescent symbol is commonly used to represent Islam.

Confucianism

Origin: China, 2,500 years ago

Leader: Kong Qiu, known as Confucius, Great Master Kong

Teachings: Followers believe in a code of living that includes goodwill, duty, manners, wisdom, and trustworthiness. They believe that the success of society depends on good and honest leaders. They do not believe in a god or an afterlife.

Sacred Book: a collection of Confucius's sayings and conversations called the Analects

Places of Worship: temples

Major Festival: Teacher's Day on Confucius's birthday, September 28

Followers: 350 million worldwide

Asian Countries Where Practiced Most: China, Japan, Korea, Taiwan, and Vietnam

Islam

Origin: Mecca (Saudi Arabia), 1,500 years ago

Leader: Prophet Muhammad, known as the Praised One

Teachings: Followers (known as Muslims) believe in one God—Allah. They also believe in five pillars: faith in Allah; prayer five times a day; fasting throughout Ramadan; charity; and travel to Mecca, the holy city, at least once in a lifetime.

Sacred Book: Qur'an (or Koran)

Places of Worship: mosques

Major Festival: Ramadan, the holy month when Muslims do not eat or drink from sunrise to sunset

Followers: 1.2 billion worldwide

Asian Countries Where Practiced Most: Afghanistan, Azerbaijan, Bahrain, Bangladesh, Indonesia, Iran, Iraq, Jordan, Kuwait, Malaysia, Pakistan, Qatar, Saudi Arabia, Turkey, United Arab Emirates, Uzbekistan, and Yemen

Major Religions of Asia

"Om" or "aum" is the main symbol of Hinduism. The symbol represents the sound heard in deepest meditation.

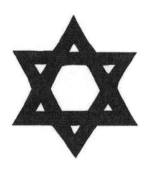

The Star of David represents the religion of Judaism. The symbol is featured on the Israeli flag.

Hinduism

Origin: India, 5,000 years ago; world's oldest religion

Leader: There is no single authority. The religion grew gradually over time.

Teachings: Followers have a wide variety of beliefs. Many Hindus believe in one or more gods, such as—Brahma, Vishnu, and Shiva. They also believe in reincarnation, in which human and animal spirits come back to Earth in different forms to live again. There is also a belief in *karma*, the idea that a person's actions in a past life determine his or her destiny.

Sacred Book: the Vedas

Places of Worship: temples

Major Festivals: More than 1,000 important festivals each year, celebrating nature's cycle and the gods

Followers: 900 million worldwide

Asian Countries Where Practiced Most: India and Nepal

Judaism

Origin: the area now called Israel, 3,700 years ago

Leaders: Abraham, Jacob, and the prophet Moses

Teachings: Followers believe in one God. Their beliefs are based on laws for conduct and worship, including the Ten Commandments, which God revealed to Moses. These laws emphasize justice, charity, honesty, and being true to one God.

Sacred Book: the Torah

Places of Worship: synagogues, also called temples

Major Festivals: Rosh Hashanah, Yom Kippur, and Passover

Followers: 12 million worldwide

Asian Country Where Practiced Most: Israel

Name _____

Major Religions of Asia

A. Find and circle the words in the word puzzle. Words may appear across, down, or diagonally.

```
A  B  B  F  I  S  D  E  E  J  R  C  B  A  C
B  E  W  I  S  L  A  M  B  P  T  H  K  T  O
M  A  G  C  B  N  E  J  L  O  O  Z  J  L  N
C  R  A  L  U  M  T  N  A  P  R  A  S  Y  F
H  E  I  Z  D  V  A  G  K  E  A  B  E  X  U
R  H  I  N  D  U  I  S  M  A  H  Y  I  H  C
I  S  B  S  H  L  E  M  T  I  R  H  R  B  I
S  I  I  N  I  M  A  I  J  T  P  M  S  T  A
T  T  B  A  S  R  I  B  N  U  S  I  A  G  N
I  I  L  L  M  K  U  K  L  I  O  I  S  Z  I
A  S  E  R  T  K  R  E  A  S  L  F  E  H  S
N  D  C  U  W  A  Y  D  I  S  E  K  U  V  M
I  A  G  W  M  X  U  O  K  P  O  N  V  H  E
T  L  T  E  V  J  U  N  A  C  O  O  R  S  A
Y  V  E  H  Z  E  M  U  S  L  I  M  X  A  D
```

Bible
Buddhism
Christianity
Confucianism
Hinduism
Islam
Judaism
karma
Muslim
Torah

B. Draw one of the religious symbols from the other pages. Write the religion it represents below the drawing. Then write three facts about that religion.

1. _____

_____

2. _____

_____

3. _____

_____

Education in Asia

Education in Asia varies greatly from place to place. Many rural areas have little access to organized schools or school materials such as textbooks. In some places, it is hard for girls and women to find educational opportunities. But in most urban areas, education is thriving. Japan and India both have some of the best education systems in Asia.

Elementary Education in Japan

School is hard in Japan, where the literacy rate (people's ability to read and write) is high compared to many countries of the world. In Japan, students go to six years of elementary school, three years of middle school, and three years of high school.

There are 20 to 30 students in a class. The main subjects taught in fourth, fifth, and sixth grades are Japanese language, math, science, social studies, music, art, and physical education. In Japanese classes, students learn to read and write 1,006 *kanji* characters (Chinese characters used in Japanese writing). They also take classes in home economics—basic cooking and sewing—and ethics. Ethics class includes manners, respect for elders, and good behavior.

The average number of days in the school year is 240. Students go to school for about seven hours a day and take five or six classes each day. Each class is 45 minutes long. The students stay in one room for most subjects, and teachers move from room to room. There are short 5- to 10-minute breaks after each class. Lunch is about 40 minutes long and there is one 20-minute recess.

Classes are divided into small teams for special activities. Each week, teams clean the classrooms, halls, and yards of their school. They tend to the plants in and around the school. Teams also take turns serving lunch to their classmates. Two hours a week are devoted to events such as sports, cultural festivals, field trips, and club meetings.

Higher Education in India

In India, *higher education*, or college, begins when students are about 18 years old and have completed primary, secondary, and senior secondary education levels. At that point, students may enter one of the more than 17,000 universities, colleges, and technical institutes in India.

Completing higher education can take anywhere from three to five years, depending on whether students want to earn a bachelor's degree in arts or science, or a degree in engineering, medicine, or law.

India is well-known for its top-notch technical institutes. At these schools, students can earn degrees in computer application, business administration, pharmacy, and hotel management.

Education in Asia

Fill in the chart, comparing your school or class with a typical school in Japan.

	Japan	Your School or Class
Length of school year and school day	240 days, 7 hours a day	
Subjects	math, social studies, science, health, Japanese language, art, music, PE, home economics, moral education	
Lunch and recess	Lunch is 40 minutes long and is usually eaten in the classroom. Students take turns serving other classmates. There is also a 20-minute recess.	
Special activities during the week	cleaning the school, tending to plants, field trips, sports, festivals, and club meetings	
Homework	every night and during vacation time	
After-school activities	clubs such as baseball, table tennis, chess, origami, computer lab, and English lessons	

Asian Cuisine

Many types of food dishes that might be familiar to you come from Asia. From spicy sauces to sweet desserts, Asian cuisine is as diverse as its different cultures.

Food	Description	Origins
Sushi	raw slices of fish, such as tuna, salmon, or yellowtail, placed over sticky rice or rolled in seaweed	Japan
Kimchi	pickled vegetables with spicy seasonings	Korea
Pad Thai	stir-fried noodles with egg, lime juice, peanuts, bean sprouts, and shrimp or chicken	Thailand
Peking duck	roasted and seasoned duck, often served with a sweet bean sauce	China
Curry	a spicy sauce made of seasonings such as turmeric, coriander, cumin, ginger, garlic, and chilies; usually served over meat and rice	India; eaten throughout Southeast Asia
Baklava	sweet, flaky pastry filled with crushed nuts and covered in honey	* Turkey; eaten throughout the Middle East
Hummus	a dip made of mashed chickpeas, sesame paste, olive oil, lemon juice, garlic, and salt and pepper	the Levant, an area that includes Syria, Lebanon, Israel, Jordan, and parts of Turkey and Palestine
Roti canai	flatbread that is typically pulled apart and eaten with the hands	Malaysia

* Not everyone agrees on the origins of baklava, but most evidence suggests that it comes from the former Ottoman Empire in Turkey.

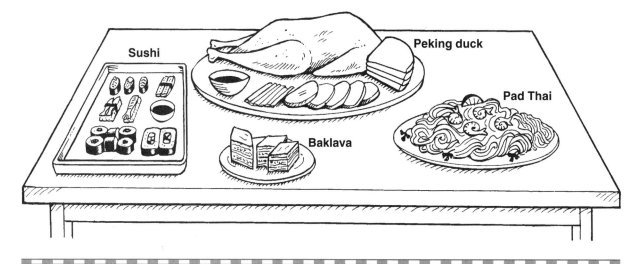

Asian Cuisine

A. Write the letter of the place that each type of Asian food comes from.

_____ 1. sushi   a. Turkey

_____ 2. curry   b. Korea

_____ 3. kimchi   c. Thailand

_____ 4. Peking duck   d. Japan

_____ 5. roti canai   e. China

_____ 6. baklava   f. the Levant

_____ 7. pad Thai   g. India

_____ 8. hummus   h. Malaysia

B. Answer the questions.

1. Have you eaten any of the Asian foods listed on the other page? If so, which ones have you eaten?

   _____

   _____

2. If you answered "yes" to number 1, which food was your favorite and why?

   _____

   _____

3. If you answered "no" to number 1, which Asian food would you most like to try? Why?

   _____

   _____

Celebrations

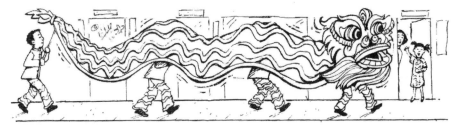

Chinese New Year

Chinese New Year is a 15-day celebration that marks the start of the new year on the Chinese calendar. The date of the festival is based on the phases of the moon. It begins on a new moon between January 21 and February 20 and ends on the first full moon 15 days later. Throughout the festival, there are parades, fireworks, and dances featuring colorful lion and dragon costumes.

The following traditions are practiced by many Chinese people to celebrate the beginning of the new year:

Before the Festival

The home is thoroughly cleaned to sweep out the old year. Then people decorate the home. Flowers, representing rebirth and new growth, are placed throughout the house. Platters of fresh and dried sweet fruit are set out for guests. Poetic messages are written on red paper and hung on walls and doors. For example, a message might say, "May you enjoy continuous good health."

New Year's Eve

On the night before the first day of the festival, families gather for a special dinner. Places are set for absent family members. Many dishes of food are served, including chicken, fish, rice, spring rolls, dumplings, and vegetables. Guests bring small gifts of oranges and tangerines, symbolizing happiness.

New Year's Day

On the first day of the festival, families pay respects to their ancestors at local temples. People visit relatives, neighbors, and friends to exchange good wishes. Children receive red envelopes filled with money to wish them good luck and wealth in the new year.

The Lantern Festival

The Lantern Festival is held on the last day of the Chinese New Year celebration and represents hope for the coming year. Lit lanterns are hung outside of homes, with riddles attached to them. Visitors who solve the riddles receive small gifts. Visitors are also given rice dumplings, which symbolize harmony and happiness. Hundreds of colorful, animal-shaped lanterns are also displayed in public areas, and children carry lanterns through the streets.

Name _____

Celebrations

Chinese New Year

According to the Chinese calendar, each new year represents one of 12 animal signs. These animals repeat in a 12-year cycle. For example, 2010 was the Year of the Tiger. The Year of the Tiger will occur again in 2022, 2034, and so on. It is said that a person born in the year of a certain animal has some of the same traits as that animal. The animal signs, their personality traits, and the years they occur are shown in a chart called the Chinese Zodiac.

Read the Chinese Zodiac and circle your sign. Does it describe your personality?

The Chinese Zodiac

Tiger 1974, 1986, 1998, 2010	Rabbit 1975, 1987, 1999, 2011	Dragon 1976, 1988, 2000, 2012	Snake 1977, 1989, 2001, 2013
Brave, smart, and a strong leader. Likes Horse and Dog. Beware of Monkey!	Happy, loving, and a good peacemaker. Likes Sheep and Pig. Beware of Rooster!	Lucky, honest, and a great adventurer. Likes Monkey and Rat. Beware of Dog!	Quiet, thoughtful, and a terrific organizer. Likes Rooster and Ox. Beware of Pig!
Horse 1978, 1990, 2002, 2014	Sheep 1979, 1991, 2003, 2015	Monkey 1980, 1992, 2004, 2016	Rooster 1981, 1993, 2005, 2017
Shy, cheerful, and a hard worker. Likes Tiger and Dog. Beware of Rat!	Wise, generous, and a talented artist. Likes Pig and Rabbit. Beware of Ox!	Clever, intelligent, and funny. Likes Dragon and Rat. Beware of Tiger!	Proud, alert, and a good public speaker. Likes Snake and Ox. Beware of Rabbit!
Dog 1982, 1994, 2006, 2018	Pig 1983, 1995, 2007, 2019	Rat 1984, 1996, 2008, 2020	Ox 1985, 1997, 2009, 2021
Dependable, honest, and a loyal friend. Likes Horse and Tiger. Beware of Dragon!	Kind, sincere, and a thoughtful teacher. Likes Rabbit and Sheep. Beware of other Pigs!	Charming, eager, and a fine inventor. Likes Dragon and Monkey. Beware of Horse!	Strong, calm, and a good listener. Likes Snake and Rooster. Beware of Sheep!

Celebrations

Hina Matsuri

In Japan, March 3 is the holiday of Hina Matsuri, also known as the Japanese Doll Festival. Hina Matsuri is a day of prayer for the health and happiness of young girls. Families with daughters celebrate this day by setting up a display of dolls inside the house and serving diamond-shaped rice cakes and tiny crackers.

The practice of setting up dolls began as a way to ward off evil spirits. In some parts of Japan, people still throw paper dolls into a river, hoping that the dolls will carry away sickness or misfortune.

Most people display their doll collection in the middle of February and put it away as soon as Hina Matsuri is over. This is because of an old superstition that says if families are too slow in putting away their dolls, their daughters will have trouble marrying!

The dolls of Hina Matsuri are dressed in the costumes of the Japanese imperial court, which was at its peak from AD 794–1192. The dolls are placed on a platform that has several *tiers*, or levels, covered in red cloth. Traditionally, people put the dolls in a specific place on each tier, though many families are beginning to change or limit the doll displays because they are very expensive.

First Tier

The emperor and empress sit at the top on the first tier. They sit in front of a gold folding screen, just like the real imperial throne of ancient Japan.

Second Tier

Three court ladies sit on the second tier, holding small cups for *sake* (sah-KEH), a rice wine.

Third Tier

Five male musicians—three drummers, a flute player, and a singer—are on the third tier.

Fourth Tier

Two ministers, or counselors of the emperor and empress, are displayed on the fourth tier. They sit on either end of a set of tables with small bowls of crackers and cakes.

Fifth Tier

The fifth tier holds three servants who protect the emperor and empress.

Celebrations

Hina Matsuri

Color the drawing of the five-tiered Hina doll set. Then write the names of the dolls that appear on each tier next to the numbers below.

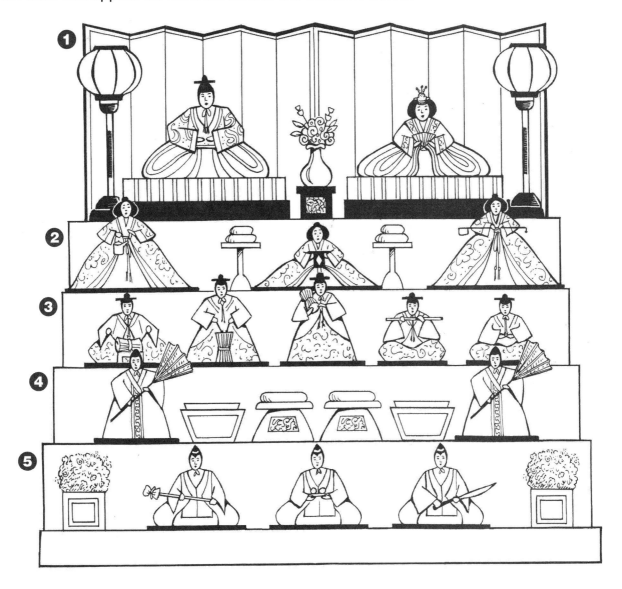

Tier 1: _____   Tier 4: _____

Tier 2: _____   Tier 5: _____

Tier 3: _____

Name _____

Review

Use words from the box to complete the crossword puzzle.

calendar

culture

Hina Matsuri

India

Japan

Petra

religions

Thailand

Across

2. The school year in _____ lasts 240 days.

4. Pad Thai is a famous dish in _____.

6. Asia is home to six major _____.

8. _____ is the languages, beliefs, arts, and traditions of a group of people.

Down

1. The Chinese _____ is based on the phases of the moon.

3. _____ is an ancient city in Jordan.

5. _____ is the Japanese Doll Festival.

7. The Bollywood film industry in _____ is the largest in the world.

Assessment

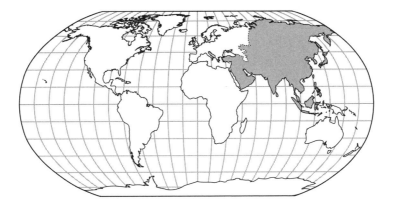

This section provides two cumulative assessments that you can use to evaluate students' acquisition of the information presented in this book. The first assessment requires students to identify selected cities, countries, landforms, and bodies of water on a combined physical and political map of Asia. The second assessment is a two-page multiple-choice test covering information from all sections of the book. Use one or both assessments as culminating activities for your class's study of Asia.

CONTENTS

Map Test

Write the name of the country, city, landform, or body of water that matches each number. Use the names in the box to help you.

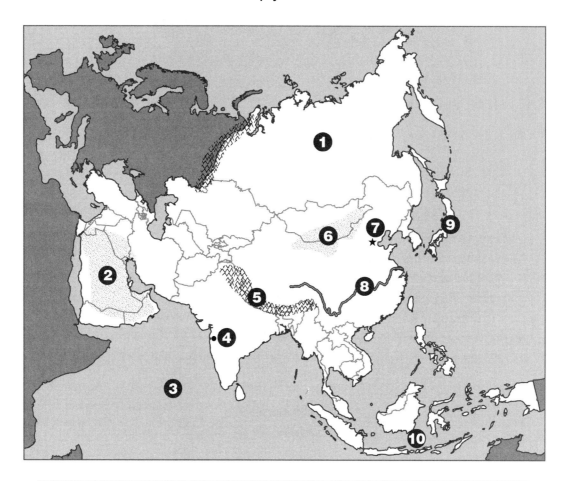

Arabian Desert	Indian Ocean	Russia	Mumbai	Himalayas
Yangtze River	Gobi Desert	Japan	Beijing	Indonesia

1. _____

2. _____

3. _____

4. _____

5. _____

6. _____

7. _____

8. _____

9. _____

10. _____

The 7 Continents: Asia • EMC 3734 • © Evan-Moor Corp.

Multiple-Choice Test

Fill in the bubble to answer each question or complete each sentence.

1. Asia is the largest continent in the world in ____.

   Ⓐ size

   Ⓑ population

   Ⓒ both size and population

   Ⓓ number of cities and countries

2. Which continent shares a land border with Asia?

   Ⓐ Europe

   Ⓑ Australia

   Ⓒ North America

   Ⓓ South America

3. In which two hemispheres is Asia mostly located?

   Ⓐ Northern and Southern

   Ⓑ Eastern and Western

   Ⓒ Southern and Western

   Ⓓ Northern and Eastern

4. Asia's ____ countries are divided into ____ regions.

   Ⓐ 20, 4

   Ⓑ 50, 6

   Ⓒ 50, 8

   Ⓓ 75, 10

5. Which country is the largest in size, but smallest in population?

   Ⓐ Qatar

   Ⓑ Nepal

   Ⓒ Russia

   Ⓓ Philippines

6. Which two countries rank first and second in population?

   Ⓐ China and India

   Ⓑ China and Japan

   Ⓒ Indonesia and Pakistan

   Ⓓ Bangladesh and Vietnam

7. Which mountain range is the highest in Asia and in the world?

   Ⓐ Mount Everest

   Ⓑ Altai Mountains

   Ⓒ Zagros Mountains

   Ⓓ Himalaya Mountains

8. The ____ Desert is the largest in Asia.

   Ⓐ Gobi

   Ⓑ Thar

   Ⓒ Arabian

   Ⓓ Taklimakan

Multiple-Choice Test

9. Which ocean does *not* border the continent of Asia?

    Ⓐ Atlantic

    Ⓑ Arctic

    Ⓒ Indian

    Ⓓ Pacific

10. The top two oil-producing countries in Asia are _____.

    Ⓐ Iran and China

    Ⓑ Iraq and Kuwait

    Ⓒ Qatar and Kazakhstan

    Ⓓ Russia and Saudi Arabia

11. Asian farmers grow over _____% of the world's rice.

    Ⓐ 20

    Ⓑ 50

    Ⓒ 90

    Ⓓ 100

12. Which of these animals can only be found in the Asian rainforest?

    Ⓐ orangutan

    Ⓑ king cobra

    Ⓒ giant panda

    Ⓓ komodo dragon

13. Why are camels, elephants, and water buffalo called *beasts of burden*?

    Ⓐ They are wild animals.

    Ⓑ They carry heavy loads.

    Ⓒ They are endangered.

    Ⓓ They work in the desert.

14. Which religion was founded in India?

    Ⓐ Islam

    Ⓑ Judaism

    Ⓒ Hinduism

    Ⓓ Confucianism

15. The date of the Chinese New Year is based on the _____.

    Ⓐ phases of the sun

    Ⓑ Chinese Zodiac

    Ⓒ Lantern Festival

    Ⓓ phases of the moon

16. A major tourist attraction in Cambodia is _____.

    Ⓐ Angkor Wat

    Ⓑ the Taj Mahal

    Ⓒ the Great Wall

    Ⓓ Petra

Note Takers

This section provides four note-taker forms that give students the opportunity to culminate their study of Asia by doing independent research on places or animals of their choice. (Some suggested topics are given below.) Students may use printed reference materials or Internet sites to gather information on their topics. A cover page is also provided so that students may create a booklet of note takers and any other reproducible pages from the book that you would like students to save.

FORMS

Name _____

Select a physical feature of Asia. Write notes about it to complete each section.

_____

(Name of Physical Feature)

Location

_____
_____
_____
_____

Interesting Facts

_____
_____
_____
_____
_____
_____
_____
_____
_____
_____
_____

Description

_____
_____
_____
_____
_____
_____
_____
_____
_____

Animals or Plants

_____
_____
_____
_____

Name _____

Draw an Asian animal. Write notes about it to complete each section.

_____
(Name of Animal)

Habitat

_____
_____
_____
_____

Endangered?   (Yes)   (No)

Physical Characteristics

_____
_____
_____

Diet

_____
_____
_____
_____

Behaviors

_____
_____
_____
_____

Enemies/Defenses

_____
_____
_____
_____

Draw an Asian tourist attraction. Then write notes about it to complete each section.

_____
(Name of Tourist Attraction)

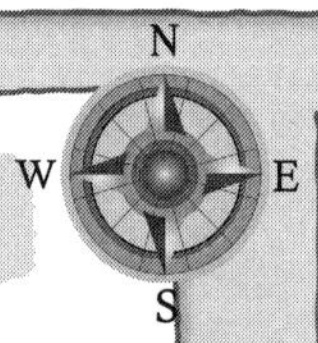

N
W E
S

Location

_____
_____
_____

Description

_____
_____
_____
_____
_____
_____
_____
_____
_____
_____
_____
_____

Interesting Facts

_____
_____
_____
_____

Name _____

Select an Asian city you would like to visit. Write notes about it to complete each section.

My Trip to _____
(Name of City)

Location

N
W · E
S

_____
_____
_____
_____

How I Would Get There

_____
_____
_____
_____

Things I Would See and Do

_____
_____
_____
_____
_____
_____
_____
_____

Foods I Would Eat

_____
_____
_____
_____

Learning the Language

How to Say "Hello"

_____

How to Say "Goodbye"

_____

Page 5

1. C 2. D 3. A 4. C 5. B

Page 6

A. Europe, Australia, southwest, Arctic, south, Pacific

B. Students should color Europe orange, use blue to circle the Pacific Ocean, and draw a kangaroo next to Australia.

Page 9

A. 1. c 2. f 3. h 4. e 5. d 6. b 7. g 8. i 9. a

B.

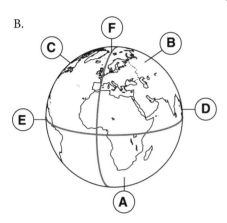

Page 11

A. 1. equator   6. latitude lines
   2. prime meridian   7. 15 degrees
   3. north   8. parallels
   4. 75°E   9. 30°N
   5. 90°N   10. meridians

B. Most places in Asia are north of the equator and east of the prime meridian.

Page 12

A. 1. No   4. No   7. Yes
   2. Yes 5. Yes 8. No
   3. No   6. No   9. No

B. Three: Asia, Australia, and Antarctica

Page 14

Across   **Down**
1. Pacific   2. Asia
5. Africa   3. Europe
6. hemispheres   4. projection
7. relative
8. equator

Page 17

1. D 2. C 3. B 4. B 5. A

Page 18

A. Answers will vary—e.g., Asia's population has been increasing steadily for the last 60 years and will continue to grow through the year 2050.

Page 19

B. 1. Yes   5. No   8. No
   2. No   6. Yes   9. Yes
   3. Yes   7. Yes 10. No
   4. Yes

C. 1. 1970–1990
   2. more than 6 billion

Page 20

Students should color Mongolia, South Korea, Sri Lanka, Turkey, and Yemen in five different colors.

B.

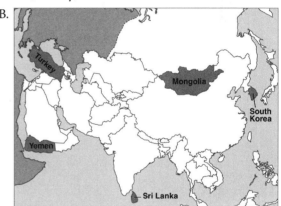

Page 22

A.

Rank	Country	Square Miles	Square Kilometers
1	Russia	4,937,800	12,788,842
2	China	3,705,407	9,596,961
3	India	1,269,219	3,287,263
4	Kazakhstan	1,052,090	2,724,900
5	Saudi Arabia	830,000	2,149,690

Page 23

B. Students should color Russia, China, India, Kazakhstan, and Saudi Arabia in five different colors.

The Five Largest Countries
1. Russia
2. China
3. India
4. Kazakhstan
5. Saudi Arabia

Page 25

A. 1. two
   2. Iran
   3. four
   4. 127 million, 669 thousand
   5. 1st: China, 10th: Myanmar
   6. Pakistan
   7. 153,215,000
   8. More: two, Fewer: eight

B. Answers will vary.

Page 26

A.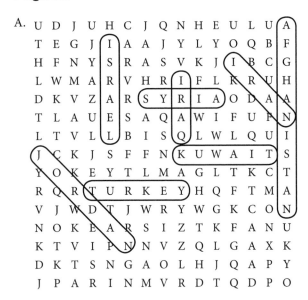

Page 27

B. Students should color the map and complete the paragraph.
   Answers will vary—e.g., Southwest Asia is sometimes called the Middle East. It is a region made up of 20 countries and about 330 million people.

Page 28

A. 1. countries
   2. billion
   3. India
   4. second
   5. Mumbai
   6. Maldives
   7. Bangladesh
   8. Sri Lanka

Page 29

B. Students should circle the Maldives in blue and color each of the other six countries a different color.
   1. Answers will vary—e.g., South Asia is made up of seven countries.
   2. Answers will vary—e.g., South Asia is one of the world's most crowded regions.
   3. Answers will vary—e.g., There are several huge cities in South Asia.

Page 30

B. 1. Kazakhstan
   2. Uzbekistan
   3. Turkmenistan
   4. Tajikistan
   5. Kyrgyzstan

Page 32

A. region, Siberia, 30, population, country, Europe, Ural, Novosibirsk

Page 33

B. Students should color the map and write a paragraph. Answers will vary—e.g., North Asia is the largest region in Asia, however, it has the smallest population.

Page 34

A. 1. Beijing
   2. Ulaanbaatar
   3. Seoul
   4. Japan
   5. Pyongyang

Page 35

B.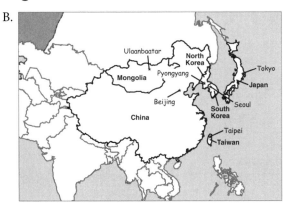

Page 36

1. Indonesia
2. Thailand
3. Laos
4. Cambodia
5. Singapore
6. Philippines
7. Brunei
8. Vietnam
9. Thailand
10. Malaysia

Page 39

A. 1. Mumbai
   2. 115,000
   3. Iran
   4. Seoul
   5. six
   6. Karachi
   7. less than 10 million

B. 1. 11
   2. 5,985,000
   3. Tianjin, Tehran, Hong Kong, and Bangkok

Page 40

Across
3. Indonesia
5. Mumbai
8. North

Down
1. Russia
2. fifty
4. South
6. billion
7. China

Page 43

1. B   2. D   3. C   4. A   5. C

Page 44

A. 1. Gobi Desert
   2. Mount Everest
   3. desert
   4. Ural Mountains
   5. West Siberian Plain
   6. north
   7. Deccan Plateau
   8. Manchurian Plain

B. Students should color the following:
   Brown: Altay Mountains, Himalaya Mountains, Ural Mountains, Zagros Mountains
   Yellow: Arabian Desert, Gobi Desert, Taklimakan Desert, Thar Desert
   Blue: Ganges River, Huang He River, Indus River, Ob River, Yangtze River, Yenisei River
   Green: Central Siberian Plateau, Deccan Plateau, Manchurian Plain, West Siberian Plain

Page 47

A. 1. No
   2. No
   3. Yes
   4. No
   5. No
   6. Yes
   7. No
   8. No
   9. Yes
   10. Yes

B. 1. about 2,500 feet
   2. 349 meters

Page 49

A. Answers will vary.
B. Answers will vary—e.g., No, because it is too dangerous to climb.

Page 51

1. water
2. continents
3. geographers
4. collided
5. peninsula
6. plates

Crack the Code
Some people think the Indian Subcontinent looks like an <u>arrowhead</u>.

Page 53

A.

B. 1. Saudi Arabia, Kuwait, Qatar, UAE, Oman, and Yemen
   2. Mongolia and China
   3. Gobi Desert
   4. Arabian Desert
   5. Arabian Desert

Page 54

A. 1. e
   2. f
   3. h
   4. c
   5. d
   6. g
   7. b
   8. a

B. Answers will vary—e.g., Siberia includes several different landforms, including frozen tundra in the north and rich steppes in the south.

Page 57

A. 1. four
   2. mountains and hills
   3. Mount Fuji, 12,388 feet
   4. over 60
   5. a group of islands
   6. A series of huge, destructive waves called tsunamis can crash along the coast.

B. Answers will vary—e.g., The mountains, waterfalls, and forests of Japan make it a very beautiful country. However, rocky peaks, deep gorges, volcanic mountains, earthquakes, and tsunamis make the islands dangerous for people.

Page 59

A. 1. tropical   5. flower
   2. monsoons   6. Malaysia
   3. humid   7. extinction
   4. tualang   8. million

B. Answers will vary—e.g.,
   1. I would like to visit because there are many different animals.
   2. I wouldn't like to visit because of the monsoons and typhoons.
   3. I would like to visit to see the world's largest flower.

Page 60

A.
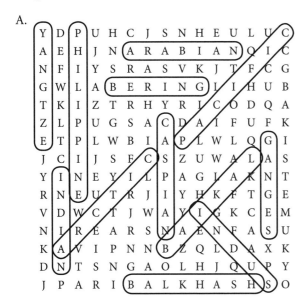

B. 1. Answers will vary—e.g., The Caspian Sea in Asia is the world's largest inland sea.
   2. Answers will vary—e.g., Asia is bordered by three oceans.

Page 63

A. 1. Caspian Sea   6. Sea of Galilee
   2. Dead Sea   7. Aral Sea
   3. Lake Baikal   8. Sea of Galilee
   4. Lake Balkhash   9. Lake Baikal
   5. Dead Sea   10. Aral Sea

B. 1. Russia
   2. Kazakhstan and Uzbekistan
   3. Lake Balkhash
   4. five
   5. Israel

Page 65

A. 1. Yangtze   5. Mekong
   2. Huang He   6. Yenisei
   3. Ganges   7. Ganges
   4. Euphrates   8. Huang He

B.

Rank	River	Length
1	Yangtze	3,900 miles
2	Huang He	3,395 miles
3	Mekong	2,600 miles
4	Yenisei	2,543 miles
5	Euphrates	1,700 miles
6	Ganges	1,560 miles

Page 66

Across	Down
4. Indian	1. Gobi
6. Siberia	2. Himalayas
7. Baikal	3. Yangtze
8. Everest	5. Dead

Page 69

1. A   2. C   3. B   4. A   5. D

Page 71

A. 1. No   6. Yes
   2. No   7. No
   3. Yes   8. Yes
   4. Yes   9. Yes
   5. No   10. No

B. 1. 420,000,000 gallons
   2. 1,590,000,000 liters
   3. A gallon is about four times larger than a liter.

Page 73

A. 1. resource   5. billion
    2. producer   6. larger
    3. energy   7. electricity
    4. consumed   8. carbon

B. 1. east
    2. 25,000
    3. north

Page 75

A.
```
A  F  B  F  I  S  D  E  E  J  R  C  B  A  Q
B  I  W  H  S  H  R  I  M  P  W  H  K  T  P
M  S  G  C  H  N  E  J  L  O  C  Z  J  L  P
C  H  A  L  E  M  S  A  M  P  A  N  S  Y  I
D  E  I  Z  L  V  A  G  M  E  O  B  E  X  O
A  R  W  O  L  H  B  V  M  C  T  Y  A  H  X
U  M  B  S  F  L  E  E  T  I  H  H  W  B  U
O  E  I  N  I  M  Z  I  T  P  S  E  T  R
P  N  G  A  S  F  I  B  E  U  W  I  E  G  C
A  I  X  L  H  K  U  K  N  O  I  D  Z  E
X  S  F  V  T  K  R  E  L  S  L  F  E  H  O
P  D  C  B  W  A  Y  F  I  S  E  K  R  V  C
R  A  N  W  M  X  C  O  K  P  O  N  V  H  E
Y  A  T  E  V  T  U  N  A  Z  C  O  R  S  A
M  V  E  H  Z  E  G  U  L  N  U  M  X  A  N
```

B. Answers will vary—e.g., Commercial fishermen use large nets to catch fish such as tuna from the ocean.

Page 76

A. Answers will vary. Each section of the circle graph should be a different color.

Page 77

B. 1. grain   4. rainfall
    2. percent   5. India
    3. paddies   6. water

Crack the Code
This grass, called <u>wild rice</u>, is native to North America and is not actually rice.

Page 79

A. 1. f   2. i   3. g   4. h   5. c   6. j   7. b
    8. e   9. a   10. d

B. **North Asia's taiga:** Answers will vary—e.g., The Siberian taiga is the largest forest in the world.
Northeast Asia's deciduous forests: Answers will vary—e.g., The ginseng root is found in Asia's deciduous forests.
Southeast Asia's rainforests: Answers will vary—e.g., Rainforests cover about one million square miles of Southeast Asia.

Page 83

A. 1. Orangutan   6. Birdwing Butterfly
    2. Giant Panda   7. Giant Panda
    3. Komodo Dragon   8. King Cobra
    4. Rhinoceros Hornbill   9. Orangutan
    5. King Cobra   10. Rhinoceros Hornbill

B. Answers will vary.

Page 85

A.

B. Answers will vary—e.g., Tigers are found only in Asia. There are about 3,200 tigers left in the wild today, and they belong to five subspecies. They are the Bengal tiger, Indo-Chinese tiger, Sumatran tiger, Siberian tiger, and South China tiger.

Page 87

A. **domesticated:** tamed
dromedary: a camel that has one hump
pack animal: an animal that carries large loads

B. 1. Camels carry people and large loads across long distances, just like ships.
    2. Water buffalo work as hard as machines and can plow knee-deep in mud.

C. Answers will vary—e.g., People call the Arabian camel the "ship of the desert" because it carries large loads and people across long distances in the sand.

Page 88

Across
1. buffalo
5. rice
6. Orangutan
8. forest

Down
2. fishing
3. dragon
4. resources
7. Tigers

Page 91

1. C   2. B   3. C   4. A   5. D

Page 93

A. 1. 1653
   2. It was carved into mountains.
   3. 5,500 miles (8,850 km) long
   4. Angkor Wat
   5. Petra
   6. to honor his wife who died
   7. a Hindu temple
   8. more than 2,000 years ago

B. Answers will vary.

Page 95

A. 1. Yes   7. Yes
   2. Yes   8. Yes
   3. No   9. No
   4. No   10. Yes
   5. Yes   11. No
   6. No   12. No

B. Answers will vary.

Page 99

A.

```
A B B F I S D E E J R C B A C
B E W I S L A M B P T H K T O
M A G C B N E J L O O Z J L N
C R A L U M T N A P R A S Y F
H E I Z D V A G K E A B E X U
R H I N D U I S M A H Y I H C
I S B S H L E M T I R H R B I
S I I N I M A I J T M S T A A
T T B A S R I B N U S A G N N
I I L L M K U K L I O I S Z I
A S E R T K R E A S L F E H S
N D C U W A Y D S E K U V M
I A G W M X U O K P O N V H E
T L T E V J U N A C O O R S A
Y V E H Z E M U S L I M X A D
```

B. Drawing and answers will vary—e.g., cross:
   1. The leader of the Christian faith is Jesus Christ.
   2. Christians worship in a church.
   3. The sacred book of Christianity is the Bible.

Page 101

Answers will vary.

Page 103

A. 1. d   2. g   3. b   4. e   5. h   6. a   7. c   8. f

B. 1. Answers will vary.
   2. Answers will vary.
   3. Answers will vary.

Page 105

Answers will vary.

Page 107

A. Colors will vary.
B. 1. the emperor and empress
   2. three court ladies
   3. five male musicians
   4. two ministers
   5. three servants

Page 108

Across
2. Japan
4. Thailand
6. religions
8. culture

Down
1. calendar
3. Petra
5. Hina Matsuri
7. India

Page 110

1. Russia   6. Gobi Desert
2. Arabian Desert   7. Beijing
3. Indian Ocean   8. Yangtze River
4. Mumbai   9. Japan
5. Himalayas   10. Indonesia

Page 111

1. C   2. A   3. D   4. B   5. C   6. A   7. D   8. C

Page 112

9. A   10. D   11. C   12. A   13. B   14. C   15. D   16. A

DAILY Geography

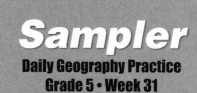
Skill: Cooperative Solutions
Essential Element 4: Standard 13

Time Zones of the United States

ANSWER KEY

Note: Not all questions can be answered with information from the map. Students will have to use their mental map skills to locate places on the map.

Monday
1. 6; Hawaiian-Aleutian, Alaskan, Pacific, Mountain, Central, and Eastern Times
2. one hour

Tuesday
1. earlier
2. Eastern Time

Wednesday
1. Hawaiian-Aleutian Time
2. 11:00 A.M.

Thursday
1. 10:00 P.M.
2. North Dakota, South Dakota, Nebraska, Kansas, and Texas

Friday
1. No, it's 2:00 A.M. and Grandfather is probably sleeping.
2. It is Daylight Saving Time.

Challenge
Answers will vary, but students should make up two questions and provide answers to the questions.

Introducing the Map

Ask students what it would be like if every community in the United States used a different time. The obvious answer is that people would be confused and many problems would be created. To avoid this confusion, a cooperative system was designed called *standard time zones*. Talk about the advantages of having regional time zones.

Explain the concept of time zones. A day is 24 hours long—the time it takes Earth to complete one rotation on its axis. Earth is divided into 24 time zones. The United States is divided into six of those twenty-four time zones.

Show students the Time Zones of the United States map. Tell students that each zone uses a time one hour different from its neighboring zones. The hours are earlier to the west of each zone and later to the east.

Go over all the names of the time zones and have students notice the one hour difference between each of them. Talk about how Alaska is so large that it covers two time zones. Explain that some of the Aleutian Islands of Alaska are so far west that scientists placed them with Hawaii, thus creating Hawaiian-Aleutian Time.

Ask students which time zone Chicago, Illinois, is in. They will probably say Central Time. Then ask them: If it is 3:00 P.M. in Chicago, what time is it in Denver? The answer is 2:00 P.M. Ask students a couple more questions, each time changing the local times to help students understand the concept.

Extend the lesson to discuss daylight saving time. This is a plan in which clocks are set one hour ahead of standard time for a certain period of time. The plan provides for an additional hour of daylight. It begins on the first Sunday in April and ends on the last Sunday in October. Most states choose to go on daylight saving time, but several don't. Talk about how that complicates things.

Introducing Vocabulary

daylight saving time a plan in which clocks are set one hour ahead of standard time for a specific period of time

standard time zone a region in which the same time is used

time zone a region in which the same time is used; Earth is divided into 24 time zones

Name

Time Zones of the United States

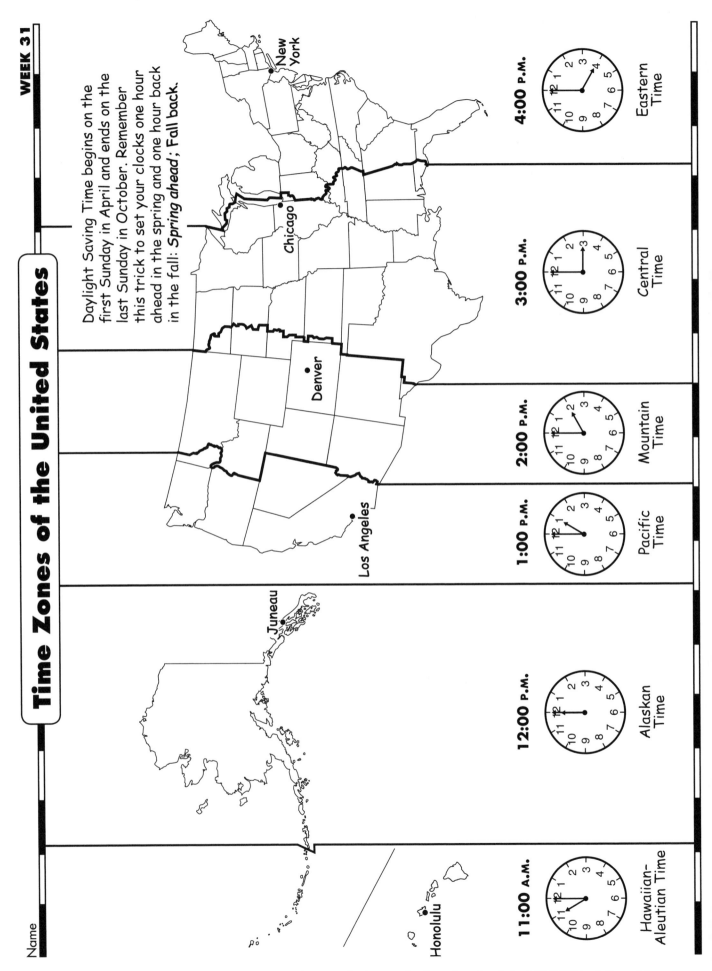

Daylight Saving Time begins on the first Sunday in April and ends on the last Sunday in October. Remember this trick to set your clocks one hour ahead in the spring and one hour back in the fall: *Spring ahead; Fall back.*

New York

Chicago

Denver

Los Angeles

Juneau

Honolulu

4:00 P.M.
Eastern Time

3:00 P.M.
Central Time

2:00 P.M.
Mountain Time

1:00 P.M.
Pacific Time

12:00 P.M.
Alaskan Time

11:00 A.M.
Hawaiian-Aleutian Time

Time Zones of the United States

Monday

1. The United States is divided into how many standard time zones? Name them from west to east.

   _____

   _____

   _____

2. What is the time difference between each neighboring time zone?

   _____

Tuesday

1. Are the hours earlier or later to the west of each time zone?

   _____

2. Cities in the Northeast region are part of which time zone?

   _____

Wednesday

1. Which time zone includes Hawaii and some of the western islands of Alaska?

   _____

2. If it is 1:00 P.M. in Chicago, what time is it in Los Angeles?

   _____

Time Zones of the United States

Thursday

1. If it is midnight in Chicago, what time is it in Seattle, Washington?

   _____

2. Which states have areas that are part of Central and Mountain Time Zones?

   _____

   _____

   _____

Friday

1. If you live in Honolulu and it is 9:00 P.M., is it a good time to call your grandfather in New York? Why or why not?

   _____

   _____

2. It is the first Sunday in April and clocks have been set one hour ahead. Why?

   _____

Challenge

Make up two time zone questions. Write your questions on the back of the map. Don't forget to include the answer. Pair up with a classmate and ask each other the time zone questions.